ORIGAMI
YOU CAN USE
27 PRACTICAL PROJECTS

RICK BEECH

ILLUSTRATED BY
RIKKI DONACHIE

DOVER PUBLICATIONS, INC.
MINEOLA, NEW YORK

Dedication

I would like to dedicate this book to my late, great father, Edwin Arthur Beech, affectionally known as "Ned," who was my first and most lasting inspiration. Paper planes with dreams on their wings, Dad.

Rick Beech

Copyright

Copyright © 2009 by Rick Beech
All rights reserved.

Bibliographical Note

Origami You Can Use: 27 Practical Projects is a new work, first published by Dover Publications, Inc., in 2009.

Library of Congress Cataloging-in-Publication Data

Beech, Rick.
    Origami you can use : 27 practical projects / Rick Beech ; illustrated by Rikki Donachie.
        p. cm.
    ISBN-13: 978-0-486-47057-3 (pbk.)
    ISBN-10: 0-486-47057-1 (pbk.)
    1. Origami. I. Title.

TT870.B4174 2009
736'.982—dc22

2008056112

Manufactured in the United States by Courier Corporation
47057102
www.doverpublications.com

Contents

Introduction

Author Rick Beech had harboured the concept of a collection of practical paperfolds for quite a few years, and it is now his great pleasure, along with illustrator Rikki Donachie, to bring you just that kind of selection, drawn from the work of creators worldwide, along with some of his own contemporary designs.

Practical origami? Why yes – all of the models in this book can be adapted for use in a variety of quirky ways, and suggestions are made here and there as to appropriate kinds of papers that would best work with given projects, which are for such as the garden, the office, the home and the dining table.

The thought process behind this collaboration (and one which kept the authors awake nights!) was trying to imagine certain situations where a piece of origami could be practically deployed, and then thinking of an appropriate design to suit; this meant considering models which might hold, support, mark, shelter, display et al, something or other!

We hope that you enjoy folding all the models we have included, and that you will have an equally fun time making use thereof.

Paper Choices

It is important when folding origami for practical use to choose paper which is strong and sturdy, and which holds a crease well. The ideal stock to use is 80–100 gsm (grams per square meter), especially if the particular design is to fulfil a practical purpose; you may be making a confetti container for a wedding or a candy holder for a party, for example.

There are many sources for such material, including art suppliers, specialist gift shops and craft markets. For the best results highly coloured and patterned paper is recommended. Be creative!

Some instructions refer to A-size paper. This is an international paper size standard that uses the metric system. Some commonly used sizes are: A4 (8.27" x 11.69"), A5 (5.83" x 8.27"), and A6 (4.13" x 5.83"). These sizes are based on a single aspect ratio of the square root of two. The proportions of A-size paper always remain the same. For example: when an A1 size paper is folded in half, it becomes the size of an A2, when an A2 is folded in half, it becomes an A3, etc.

For more detailed information on how to strengthen paper see page 93.

Thanks and Acknowledgements

The authors would like to express their heartfelt thanks and gratitude to the following creators for allowing their original origami work to be re-diagrammed and presented in this book:

Larry Hart for his Picture Frame and Business Card Holder
Gay Merrill Gross for her Butterfly page Corner
Francis Ow for his Tissue Box
David Mitchell for his Curvy Bowl
Martin Donachie-Woodrow for his Diamond Heart Name Place Holder
Carmen Sprung for her Gift Bag

Thanks also to Helen Simpson for helping proofread

And special thanks go to Gaye Woollard, a complete origami novice, who test folded all the designs and gave valuable feedback and suggestions for improvements to the diagrams and text.
Gaye is a talented photographer whose website can be found at *www.gayesart.com*

Guide to Symbols

———————————————————————— Edge of paper or edge of fold

– – – – – – – – – – – – – – – – Valley Fold

·—··—··—··—··—··—··—· Mountain Fold

———————————————— Previously made crease

··· X-ray line of a significant edge

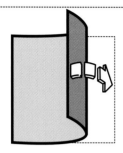

Lay paper light side up.

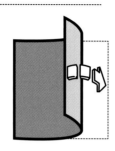

Lay paper light side down.

Unfold the indicated flap
(check next step for result).

Fold in this direction.

Fold and Unfold.

Collapse on the indicated creases.

Revolve paper in the indicated direction.

Turn the paper over.

After completing this step, the model will not lie flat.

Repeat step on other side of paper.

The next step is enlarged for clarity.

Hold the paper here.

Distance between 2 points.

4

Dividing an edge into thirds

For many origami designs we need to divide an edge accurately into thirds. The following method is convenient and accurate enough for most instances. With a bit of practice you will soon be able to do it very easily.

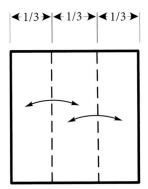

This is what the diagram might look like. Do not fold anything yet.

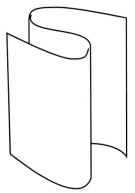

This is what you do...
Gently curve the paper into an "S" shape. We will concentrate on the top edge for the next step.

Roll the paper until the edges line up with the curves.

When the edges are lined up with the folds pinch at the edges.

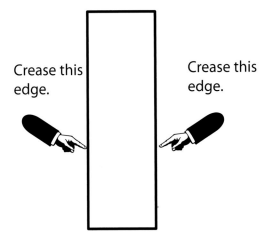

Lay the paper down flat and crease carefully and firmly along both edges.

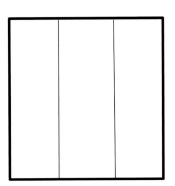

When you open up the paper, it should look like this.

Dividing an edge into fifths

Some origami designs need to divide an edge accurately into fifths. The following method was devised by the Japanese mathematician Shuzo Fujimoto.
When making the pinches, make them as small as possible, approx 5-10 mm ($^3/_{16}$" - $^3/_8$").

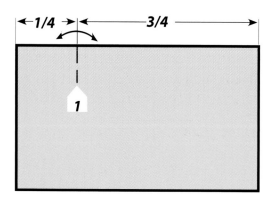

1. Make a small pinch, No. 1, at ¼ the length to be divided.

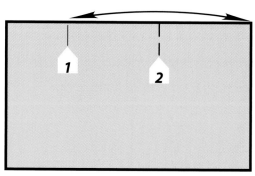

2. Divide the right-hand length in half by bringing the right-hand edge to Pinch No. 1, and make Pinch No. 2.

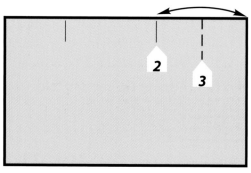

3. Divide the new right-hand length in half by bringing the right-hand edge to Pinch No. 2, and make Pinch No. 3.

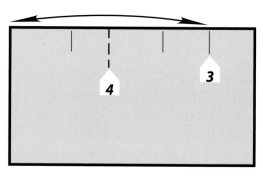

4. Divide the new left-hand length in half by bringing the left-hand edge to Pinch No. 3, and make Pinch No. 4.

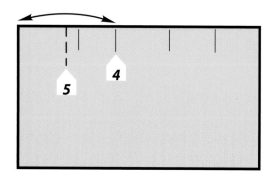

5. Divide the new left-hand length in half by bringing the left-hand edge to Pinch No. 4, and make Pinch No. 5.

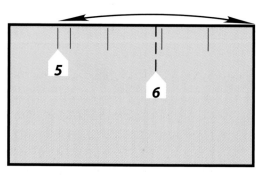

6. Divide the new right-hand length in half by bringing the right-hand edge to Pinch No. 5, and make Pinch No. 6.

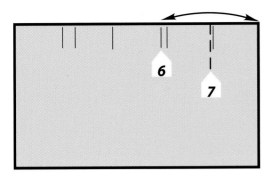

7. Divide the new right-hand length in half by bringing the right-hand edge to Pinch No. 6, and make Pinch No. 7.

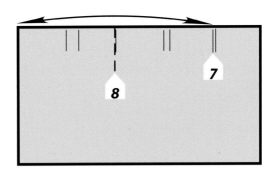

8. Divide the new left-hand length in half by bringing the left-hand edge to Pinch No. 7, and make Pinch No. 8. **Note:** Pinch No. 8 is at $\frac{2}{5}$ the length.

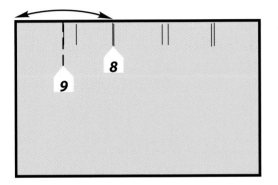

9. Divide the new left-hand length in half by bringing the left-hand edge to Pinch No. 8, and make Pinch No. 9. **Note:** Pinch No. 9 is at $\frac{1}{5}$ the length.

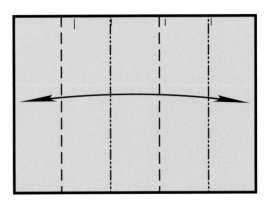

10. Using pinches 8 and 9, zig-zag fold the other creases to finish dividing the paper into fifths.

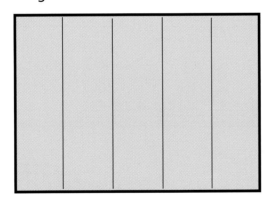

11. Equal fifths.

If one chooses the first fold to be at ¼ the length to be divided, one will discover that one's 8th and 9th pinches are at $\frac{2}{5}$ and $\frac{1}{5}$ of the length, respectively.

In origami, the larger the piece of paper, the more noticeable folding innaccuracies will be. But for most purposes in this book, the 8th and 9th pinches will suffice. A sheet of A3 will need one to continue making pinches to the 12th and 13th, A2 will require continuing to the 14th and 15th pinches, etc.

It is interesting to note that **it does not actually matter** where the first pinch is made, just continue making the pinches as shown and you will end up, eventually, with fifths.

If you are interested in the mathematics behind this, simply type - ***Fujimoto Approximation*** -into any search engine.

As unlikely as it sounds, this cup can be used to drink from. For a more robust cup choose waterproof paper, greaseproof paper or even baking foil.

Drinking Cup

Traditional

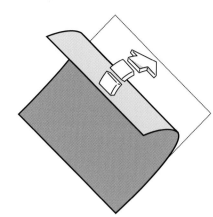

1. Lay a square light side down.

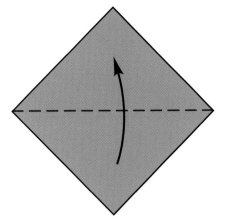

2. Valley fold upwards across the diagonal.

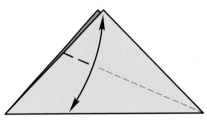

3. Fold the top corner down to the bottom edge as shown and make a pinch.

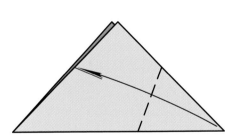

4. Valley fold the right-hand corner across so that the tip just touches the pinch made in step 3.

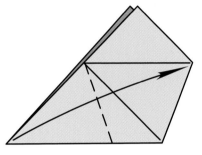

5. Valley fold the left-hand corner across as shown.

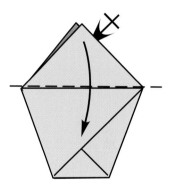

6. Valley fold the front top flap down and repeat behind.

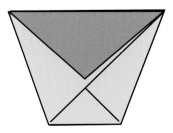

7. The finished cup. Open out the upper folded edge and fill with chosen liquid.

Dollar Wallet

by Rick Beech

You will need a European A4 or American letter size sheet of paper. Leatherette stock with a contrasting reverse colour makes a lasting carrier for your money! Begin with the textured or patterned surface face down.

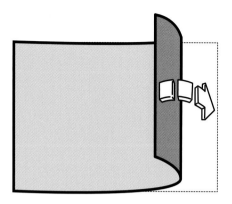

1. Lay the paper dark side down.

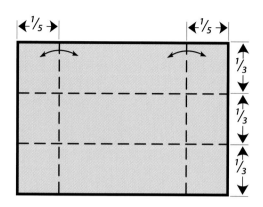

2. Precrease into fifths and thirds as shown. See pages 5-7.

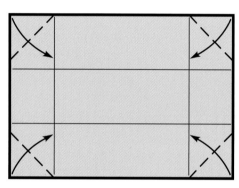

3. Valley fold all four corners in.

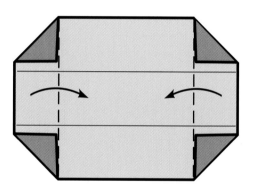

4. Valley fold the sides in.

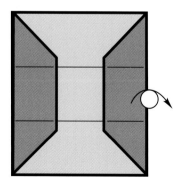

5. Turn the paper over.

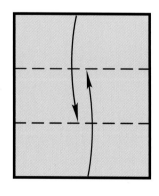

6. Valley fold the top and bottom in and tuck one into another. See next picture.

7. Stuff your wallet full of money and fold in half.

This ingenious creation holds a regular 6" x 4" photograph or postcard, with a very clever stand at the rear incorporated into the folding sequence! Use a European A4 sheet of sturdy paper such as parchment; a slight adjustment to the size of the photo is required if using American letter size paper. Begin pattern side face down.

Picture Frame

by Larry Hart

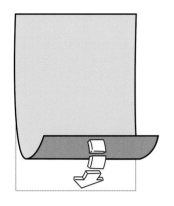

1. Lay the paper patterned side down.

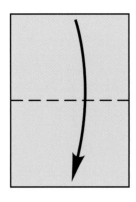

2. Fold in half downwards.

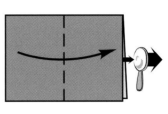

3. Fold in half from left to right.

4. Precrease the right-hand corner and repeat behind.

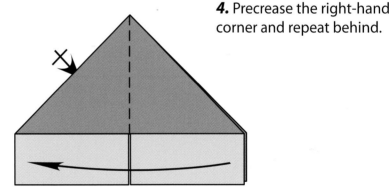

6. Swing the right-hand flap across, like the page of a book.
Repeat behind.

5. Swing the nearest flap over to the left and squash the corner down.
Repeat behind.

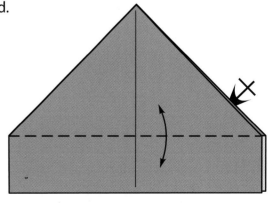

7. Crease the bottom edge up as shown.
Repeat behind.

11

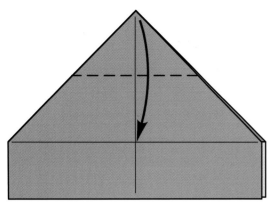

8. Fold the top corner down to meet the intersection of the previously made creases.

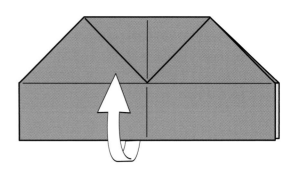

9. Lift the bottom flap up and begin to open the paper. See the next 2 steps.

9a. Keep opening the paper up.

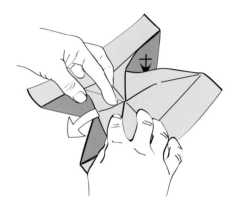

9b. To completely flatten the paper, squash the centre flaps down in the same way as the squash in step 5.

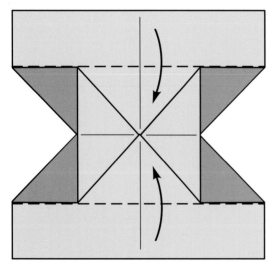

10. The paper flattened. Make sure that everything is symmetrical and lined up nicely.
Valley fold the top and bottom edges in on the creases.

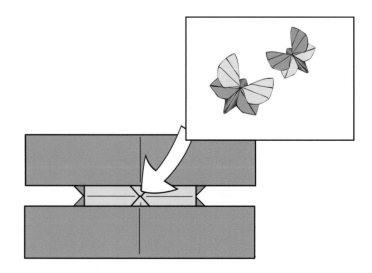

11. Place the chosen photograph centrally on top of the paper.

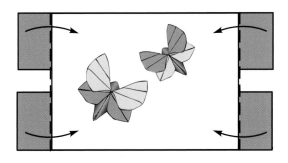

12. Valley fold the 4 tabs over the edges of the photograph.

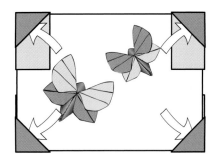

13. Tuck the corners of the photograph into the triangular pockets.
The bottom 2 corners are shown tucked in.
The triangular flap at the back can be used as a stand for landscape format pictures.

Stand for Portrait Format

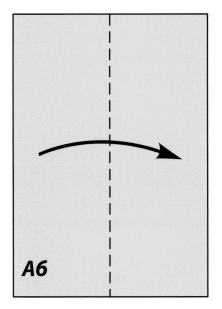

A6

14. To make a stand to use the frame in portrait format take a piece of paper that is A6 in size. Fold in half from left to right.

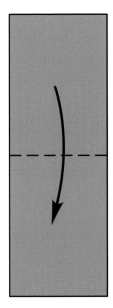

15. Valley fold in half downwards.

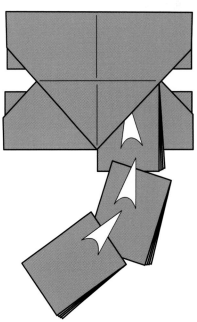

16. Insert the stand into the triangular flap at the back of the frame as shown.

13

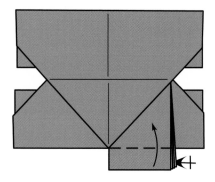

17. Valley fold the bottom edges up in line with the point of the flap. Repeat behind.

18. Remove the stand from the frame and valley fold the corner as shown. Repeat behind.

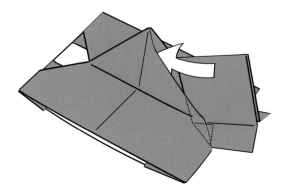

19. Carefully insert the stand into the pocket as shown and push it in as far as it will go.

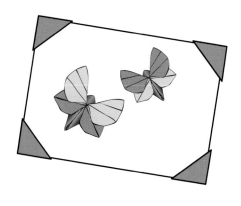

20. The finished frames, displaying your favourite pictures.

This wonderful traditional Chinese fold was one of the first that author Rick taught professionally to a group, whom he later discovered were called "The Lighthouse Fellowship"!
Use a long strip of approximately 3:1 thin, crisp paper.

Lighthouse Bookmark

Traditional - Chinese

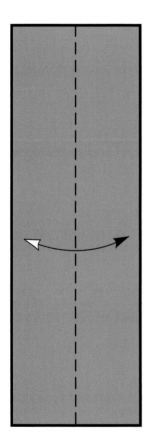

1. Begin with a 3:1 strip of lighthouse coloured paper. Crease lengthways.

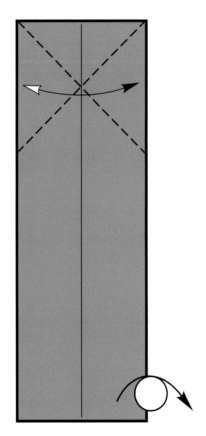

2. Valley fold diagonally from both top corners. Turn the paper over.

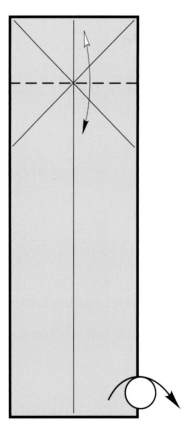

3. Valley fold horizontally as shown. Turn the paper over.

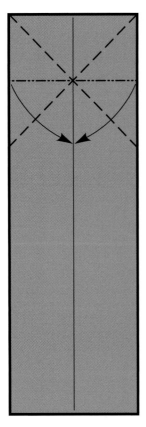

4. Collapse the paper using existing creases. This move is often referred to as a ***Waterbomb Base.***

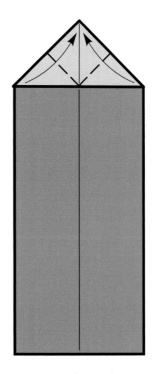

5. Valley fold the two points up to the top.

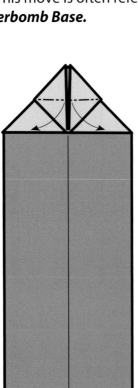

6. Open up each point and squash downwards to form two little squares.

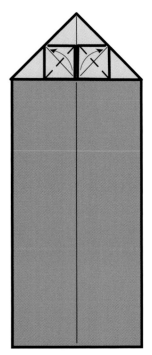

7. Valley fold the central corners outwards and upwards as shown.

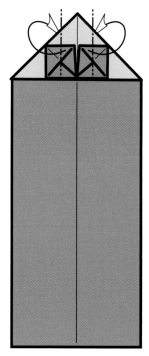

8. Mountain fold the edges of the "house" behind. The edges meet the vertical centre.

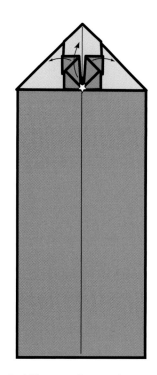

9. Lift up the point marked with a star while pulling the central parts apart to make the balcony - See next picture.

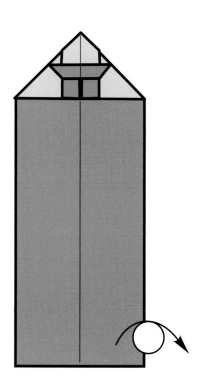

10. Turn the paper over.

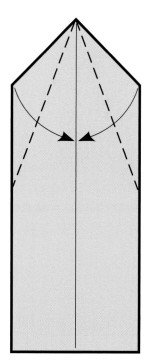

11. Valley fold the top point edges into the centre.

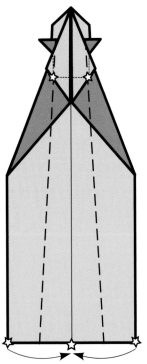

12. Valley fold the sides in as shown. The bottom corners meet on the centre line while the valley folds pass through the upper points marked with a star.

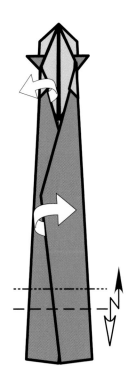

13. Make a zig-zag fold as shown and then open back out to Step 12.

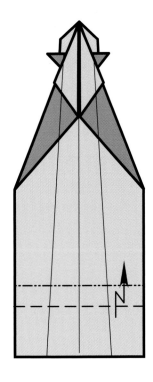

14. Remake the zig-zag fold from Step 13 straight across.

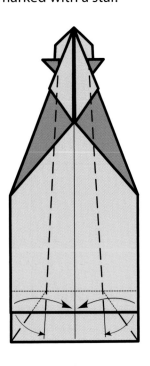

15. Remake the valley folds from Step 12 and angle the bottom as shown. See next picture.

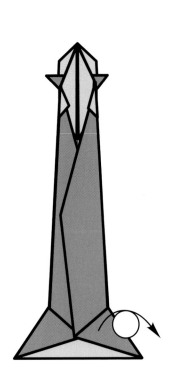

16. Turn the model over.

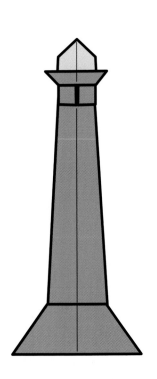

17. The finished lighthouse bookmark.

A delightfully simple design perfect for enclosing those special gifts. Choose sturdy wrapping paper or unusual handmade paper. A 600 mm/24" square will produce a bag about 200 mm/8" high.

Gift Bag

by Carmen Sprung

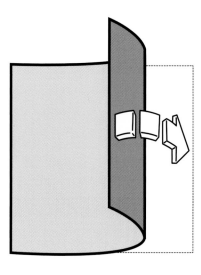

1. Lay the paper coloured side down.

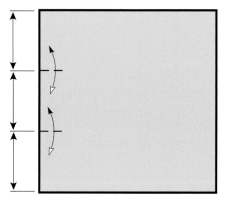

2. Divide the left-hand edge into thirds (see page 5) and make pinches.

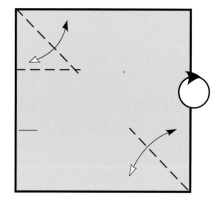

3. Crease the diagonals as shown, making sure that they intersect with the thirds creases from Step 2. Rotate the paper by 45°.

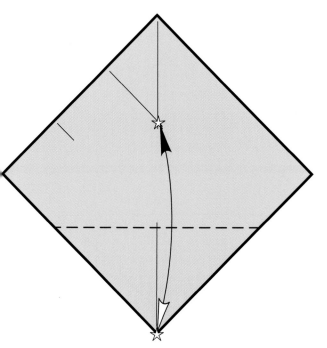

4. Lift the bottom corner and bring to touch the intersection marked with a star.

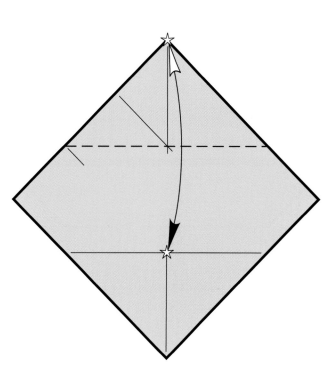

5. Repeat Step 4 with the top corner.

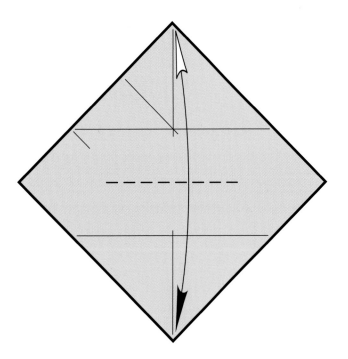

6. Valley crease in half. Only crease the central third.

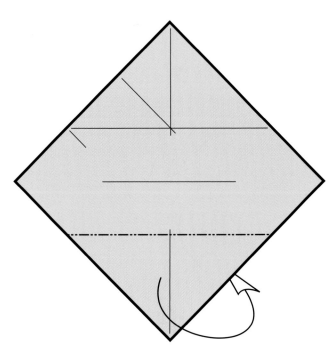

7. Mountain fold the bottom corner behind on the crease made in Step 4.

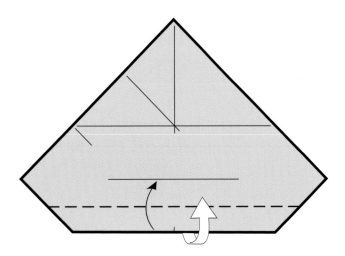

8. Valley fold the bottom edge to the middle crease allowing the corner at the back to flip forward.

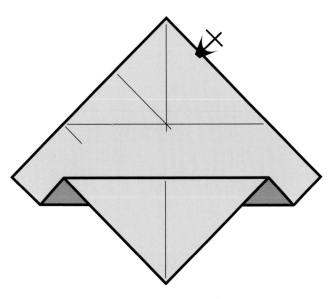

9. Repeat Steps 7 & 8 on the top corner.

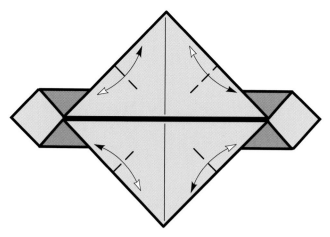

10. Valley crease the central square in half at each edge, making large-ish pinches.

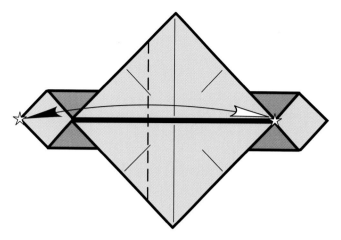

11. Bring the left-hand point over to the star and crease all the way across, ensuring that the crease intersects with the pinches made in Step 10.

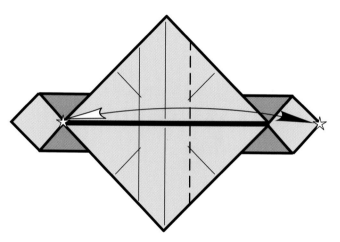

12. Repeat Step 11 with the right-hand point.

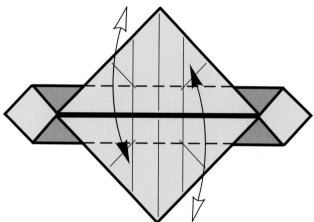

13. Valley crease the upper and lower triangles as shown.

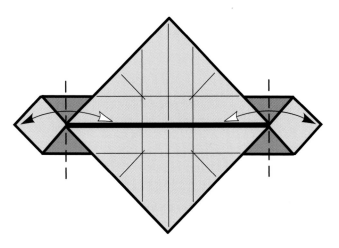

14. Valley crease the left and right-hand ends as shown.

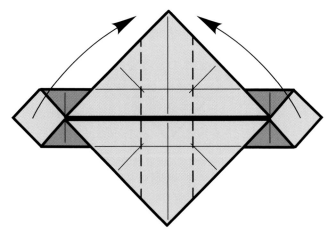

15. The precreasing is complete. Now to shape the bag. Lift each side up by 90°.

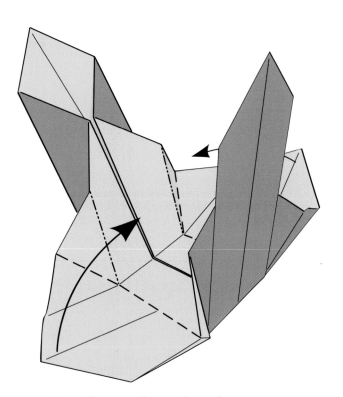

16. Lift up the sides shown making sure that you have little triangular "wings" at each corner.

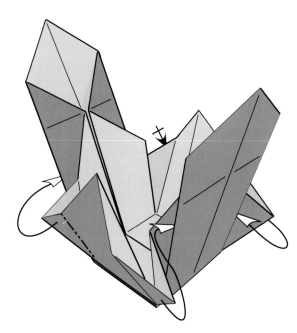

17. Tuck each of the "wings" into the pocket at the sides.

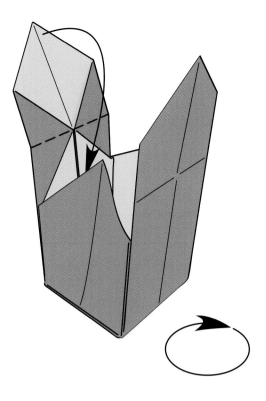

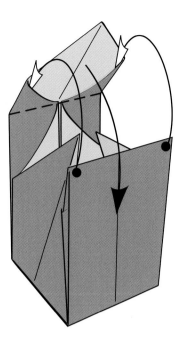

18. Fold one side down on the valley crease tucking it inside tightly. Rotate the bag by 180°.

19. Fold the other side down on the valley crease and tuck the corners marked with black dots into the pockets on the flap.

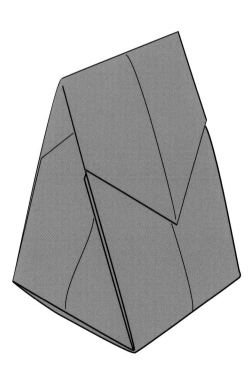

20. The perfect gift bag is now complete.

Vase

by Rick Beech

Use a large square (50 - 60 cm makes a model of ideal height to contain a small spray of flowers); heavy marbled stock with a contrasting coloured reverse side makes the perfect model!
Begin with the outer patterned side face down. Note how a coin or similar can be inserted into the model prior to the final twist movement in step 13, thus adding weight to the base.

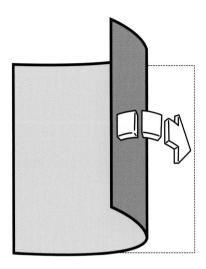

1. Begin with the outer coloured or patterned side down.

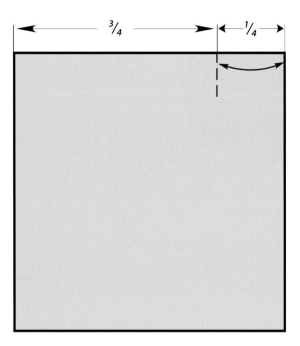

2. Make a small pinch on the top edge ¼ of the distance in from the right.

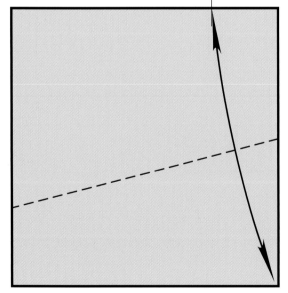

3. Bring the bottom right-hand corner to meet the pinch made in step 2 and make a valley crease right across.

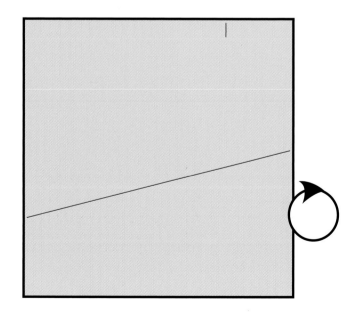

4. Rotate the paper clockwise by 90°.

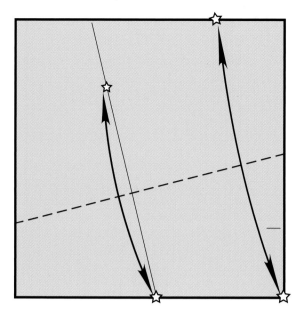

5. Make a valley crease by matching the starred points.

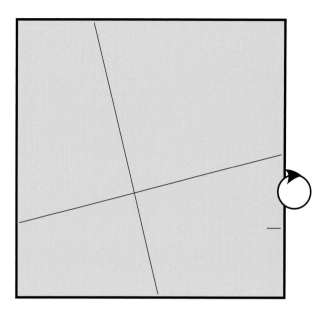

6. Rotate the paper clockwise by 90°.

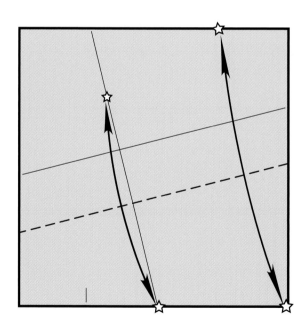

7. Make a valley crease by matching the starred points.

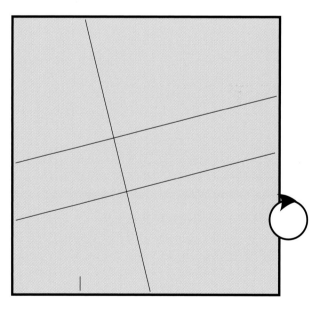

8. Rotate the paper clockwise by 90°.

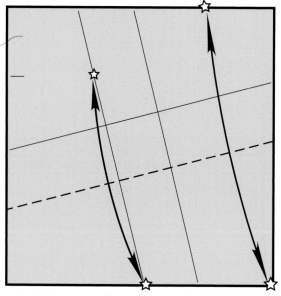

9. Make a valley crease by matching the starred points.

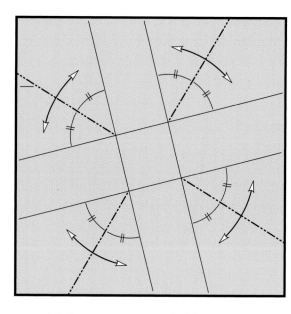

10. Make mountain fold creases on the angle bisectors as shown.

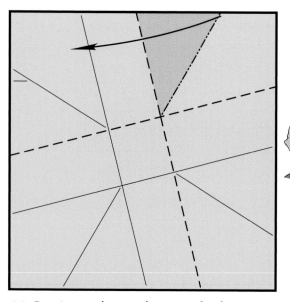

11. Begin to shape the vase by bringing the shaded area over to the left.
From here on the paper will not lie flat.

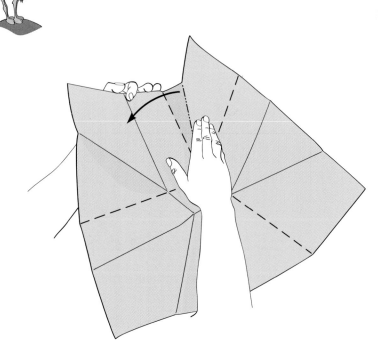

12. Step 11 in progress.

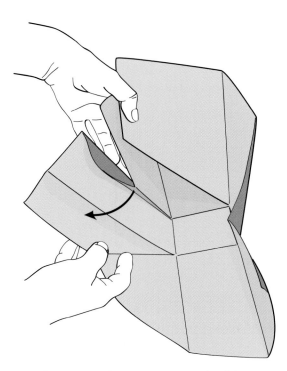

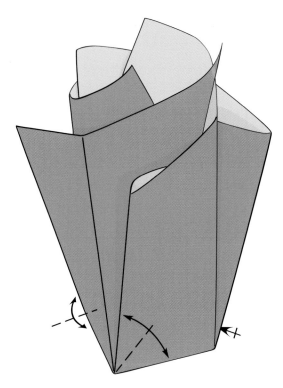

13. After completing step 10 hold it together with one hand and bring the next corner around. This is a little awkward!

14. Continue repeating step 10 on each side until you have a square cylinder as shown. Valley crease the bottom corners at 45° and twist the vase base counter-clockwise.

15. The finished vase ready for a spray of dried flowers.

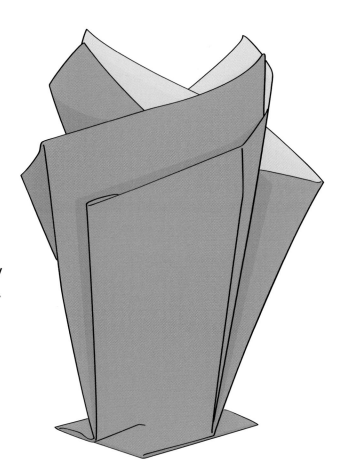

Tissue Box

by Francis Ow

This is an elegant and simple box to keep tissues handy.
Because the box is nearly 2:1 in proportion it will be perfect to store square tissues/napkins.
To get the correct size of starting square, multiply the length of the side of the tissue by 2·3.

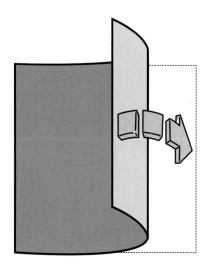

1. Begin with a large square, coloured side up.

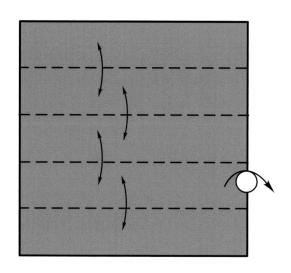

2. Divide into horizontal fifths. (See page 6.)
Turn paper over.

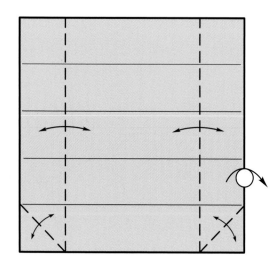

3. Valley crease the corners and the two verticals as shown.
Turn paper over.

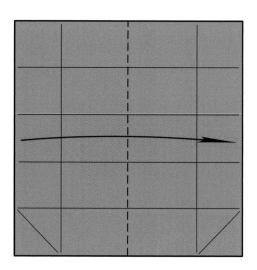

4. Fold in half from left to right.

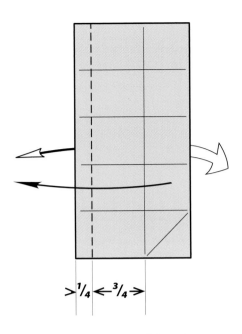

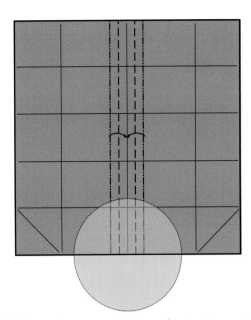

5. Fold front and back as shown. Then open out flat, coloured side up.

6. Bring the creases made in Step 5 into the middle. The next few steps will concentrate on the highlighted area.

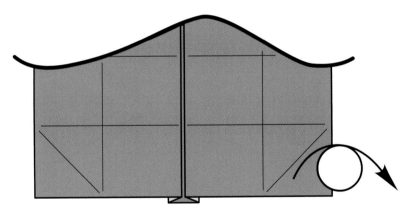

7. If your paper looks like this, turn it over.

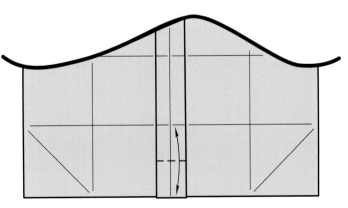

8. Make a valley crease in the central panel as shown.

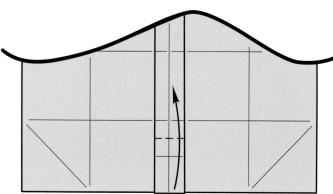

9. Valley fold the central panel up, do not crease the paper on either side.

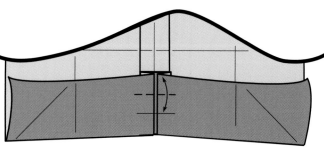

10. Valley crease exactly halfway between the edge and the crease made in Step 8.

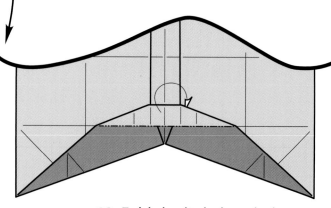

11. Using the point marked with a star as a pivot, fold the centre down making mountain folds as shown. There will be creases on the dotted triangle. See next picture.

12. Fold the little hooded part back over itself.

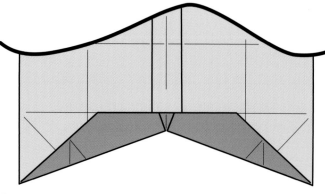

13. Repeat Steps 8-12 at the other end of the paper.

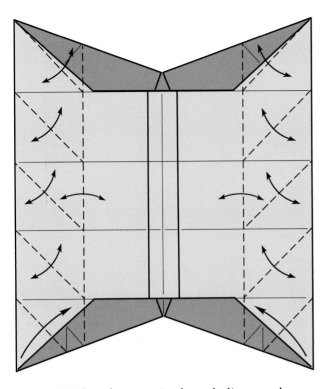

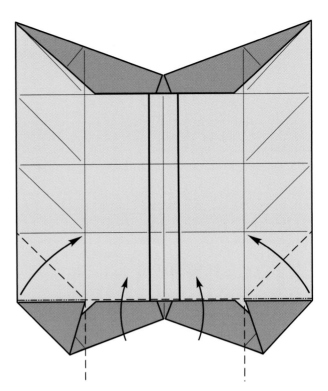

14. Make the vertical and diagonal valley crease as shown.
Valley fold the two bottom corners up and take note of them, we will be using them in Step 19 later.

15. Bring each side in as shown to make the first sides of the box.
The paper will not lie flat from this point on.

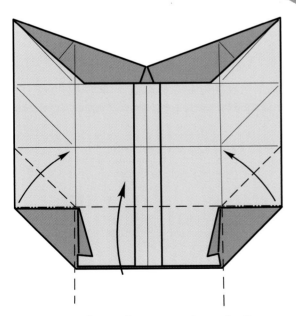

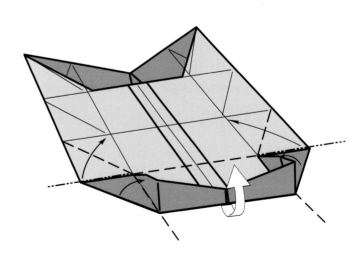

16. Bring the sides in again as before...

16a. A 3-D view of Step 16.

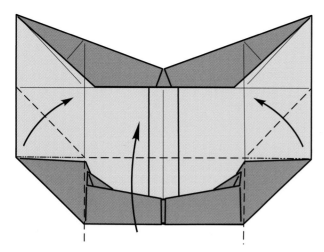

17. ...and again.

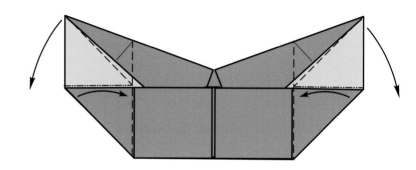

18. Bring the final sides in as before and make sure the box looks like the next picture.

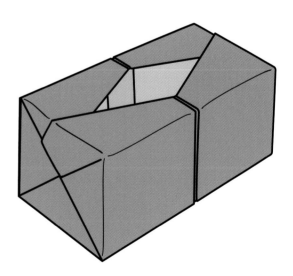

19. Open up the top front of the box and slip the points with stars underneath the flaps made in Step 14 earlier.

Tidy everything up using your fingertips through the top diamond shaped opening.

20. The finished tissue box.

Origami You Can Use ...

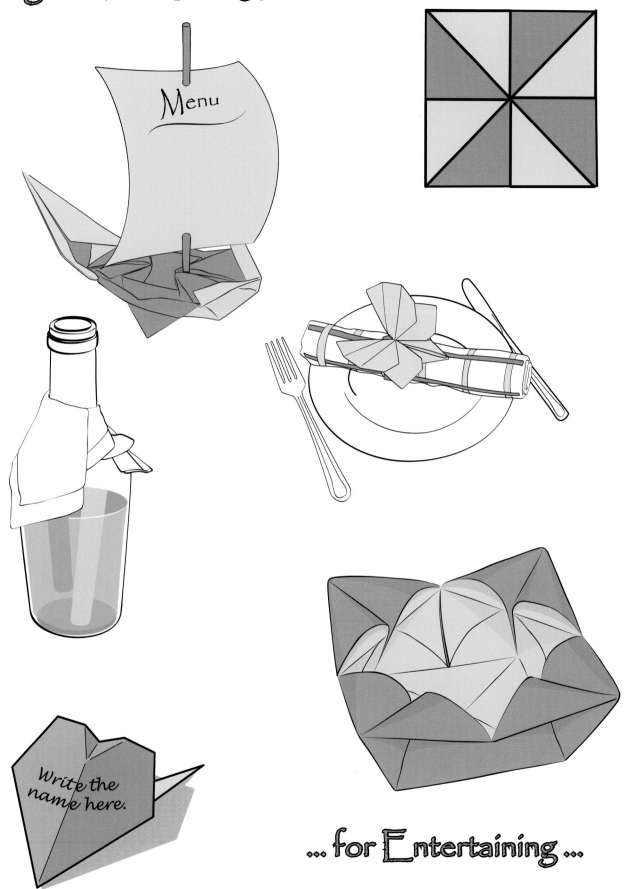

Menu

Write the name here.

Harlequin Drinks Coaster

by Rikki Donachie

A simple and colourful modular design which locks firmly together without using glue. Make a whole set in rainbow colours and brush on a couple of coats of dilute PVA (see page 93) to make them hard wearing.

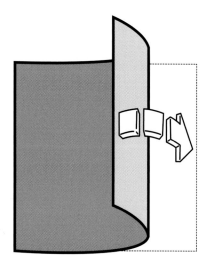

1. Start with a square coloured side up.

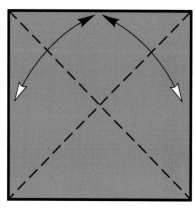

2. Valley fold both diagonals.

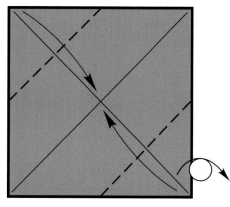

3. Fold opposite corners to the centre. Turn the paper over.

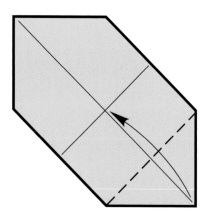

4. Fold the bottom right corner to the centre.

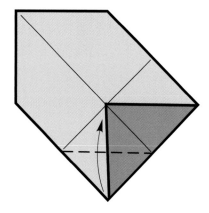

5. Fold the bottom corner up to the centre.

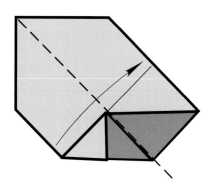

6. Valley fold in half.

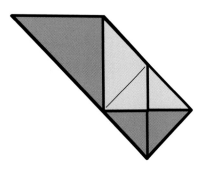

7. Repeat steps 1 - 6 with another three sheets of paper.

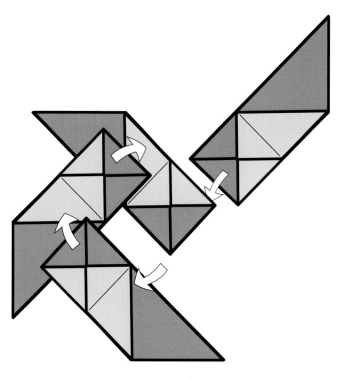

8. Interweave the square ends as shown.

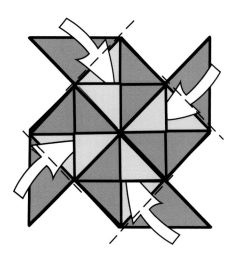

9. Valley fold the dark triangles over the edge and tuck under the light triangles.

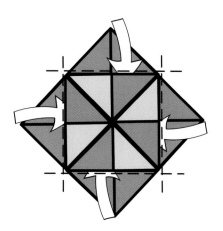

10. Valley fold the dark triangles over the edge and tuck into the pockets.

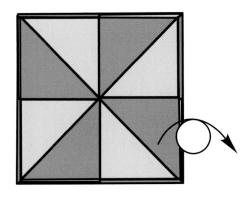

11. Turn the coaster over.

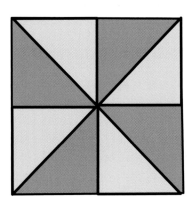

12. The finished coaster.

Diamond Heart Name Place Holder

by Martin Donachie-Woodrow

At your next dinner party consider using this elegant design for name place holders.

This simple but effective fold shows an unusual treatment of a waterbomb base.

Martin is a keen origamist and was only 7 years old when he came up with this design.

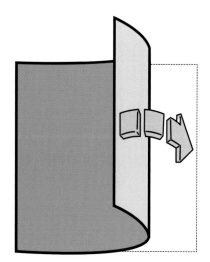

1. Start with a square coloured side up.

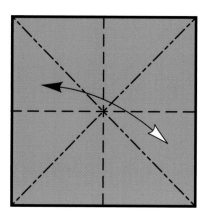

2. Precrease as shown.

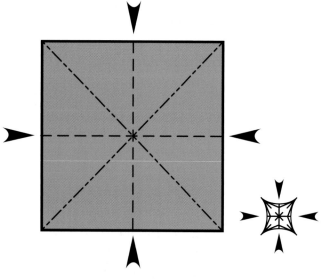

3. Collapse on the creases made in Step 2 earlier. This will result in a Waterbomb Base.
Turn the Waterbomb Base around to look like the next step.

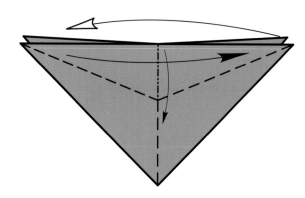

4. Fold the top front edge down as shown while swinging the left-hand point over to the right. Swing the back right corner over to the left.

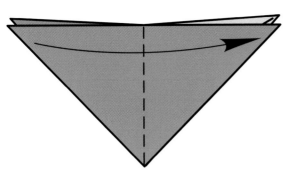

5. Swing the left point over to the right.

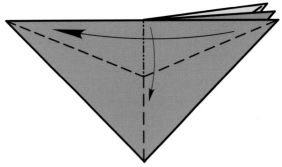

6. Fold the top front edge down as shown while swinging the right-hand point over to the left.

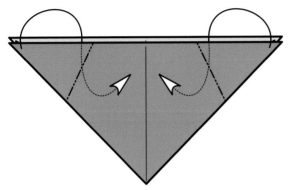

7. Inside reverse fold the two near points as shown.

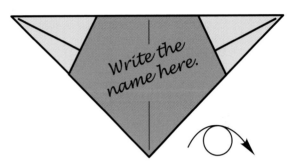

Write the name here.

8. At this point, while the model is still flat, you can write the person's name. Then turn the model over.

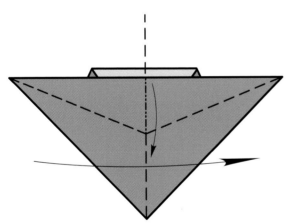

9. Fold the top front edge down as shown while folding the entire model in half.

...e the ...e here.

10. Inside reverse fold the indicated corner. Open out the model slightly.

Write the name here.

11. The finished name place holder.

Sailing Boat Menu Holder

Traditional

This is a rather fun variant of an old traditional Chinese design. Perfect for displaying the menu at a nautically-themed soireé. Choose fairly thick paper at about 300 mm/12" square.

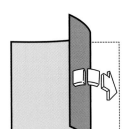

_1._ Start with a square coloured side down.

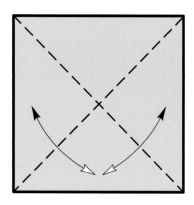

_2._ Valley crease diagonally.

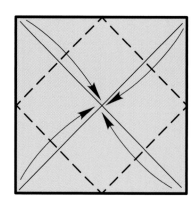

_3._ Valley fold the corners to the centre. This is known as a **_Blintz Fold_**.

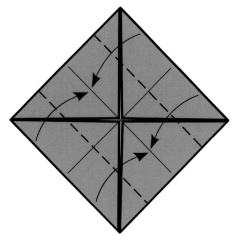

_4._ Valley fold opposite sides to the centre.

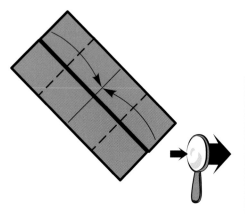

_5._ Valley fold the other two opposite sides to the centre. The next picture has been enlarged.

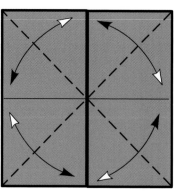

_6._ Valley crease the flaps at the corners as shown.

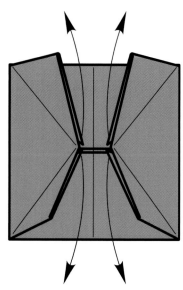

_7._ Lift the flaps and pull out the corners beneath - See next picture.

38

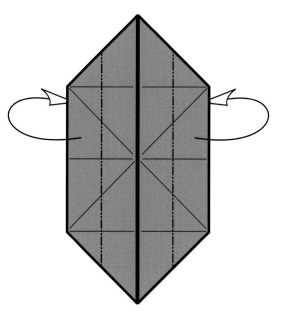

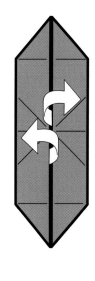

9. Open the middle edges and flatten the model - See next picture.

8. Mountain fold the sides behind.

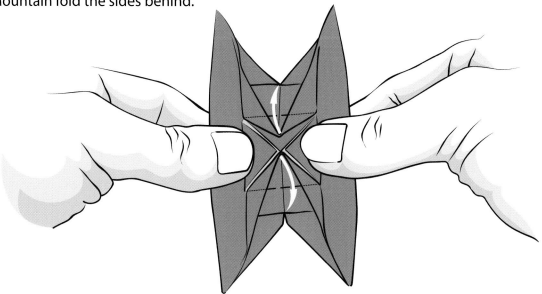

10. Squash the indicated points in the direction of the white arrows.

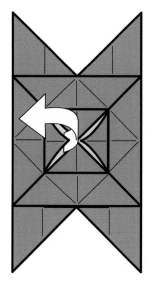

11. Lift the left-hand corner as shown and gently pull out - See next picture.

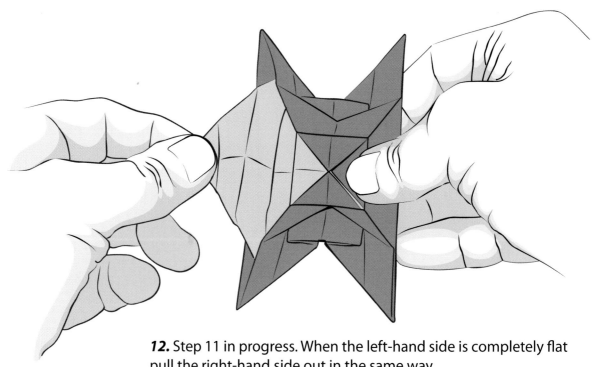

12. Step 11 in progress. When the left-hand side is completely flat pull the right-hand side out in the same way.

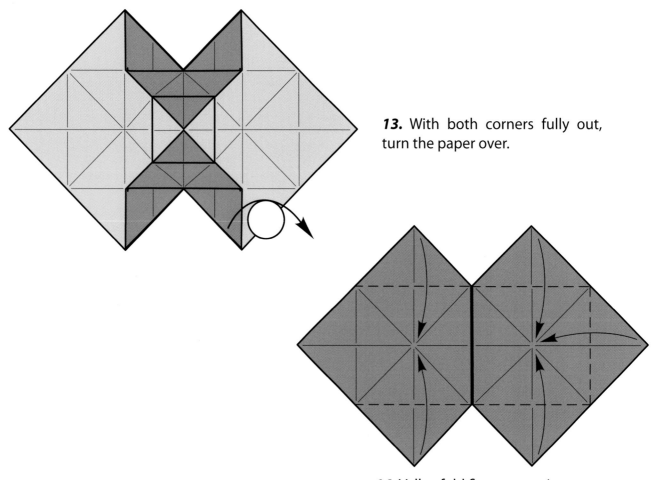

13. With both corners fully out, turn the paper over.

14. Valley fold five corners in.

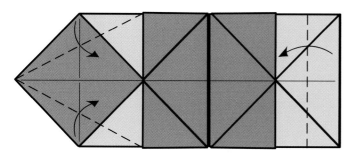

15. Valley fold where shown.

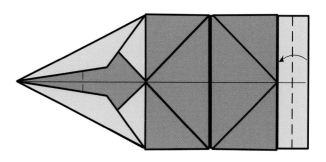

16. Valley fold right-hand side.

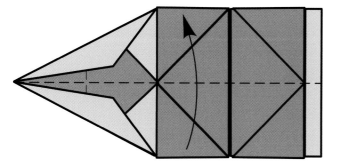

17. Valley fold in half.

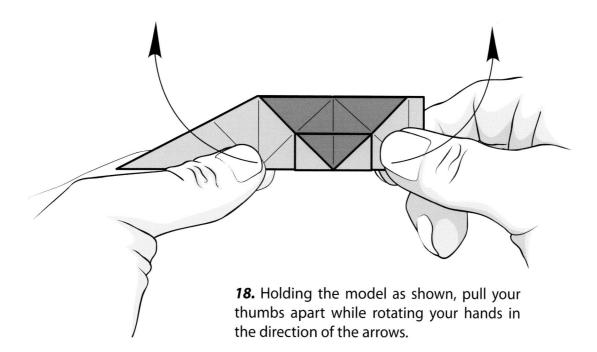

18. Holding the model as shown, pull your thumbs apart while rotating your hands in the direction of the arrows.

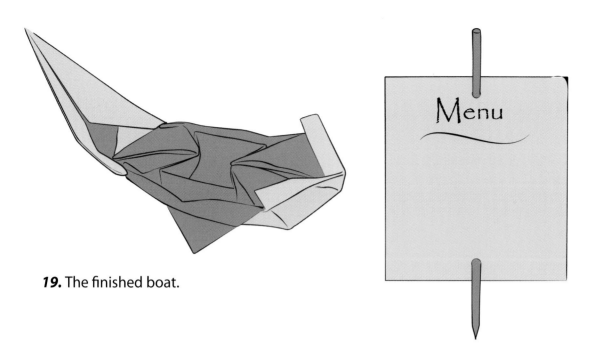

19. The finished boat.

20. Write the menu on a suitably sized piece of paper and thread a small wooden skewer through it as shown. Then insert bottom of skewer into the boat as indicated in the next picture.

21. This also works well with paper coloured the same on both sides.

Catch the drips when pouring wine to save your elegant linen tablecloth from staining.
Start with a plain white paper napkin approximately 13" or 330 mm square.
Crease diagonally in half both ways.

Wine Bottle Bib

by Rikki Donachie

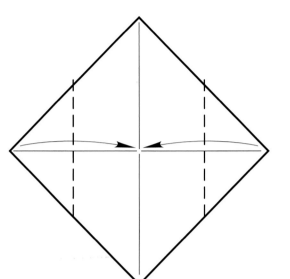

1. Fold the left and right corners into the middle.

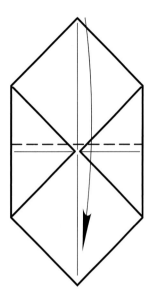

2. Fold the top corner down towards the bottom corner leaving a gap. See next picture.

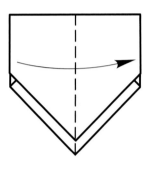

3. Fold in half from left to right.

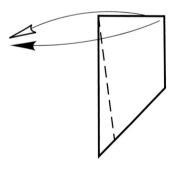

4. Fold the corners down at a slight diagonal on either side.

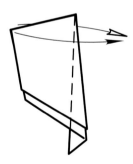

5. Fold the corners back on the vertical beneath on either side.

6. Swing the top layers over to the left, see next picture.

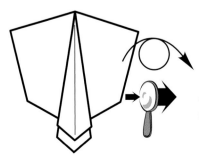

7. Turn over.
(Next pictures are enlarged for clarity.)

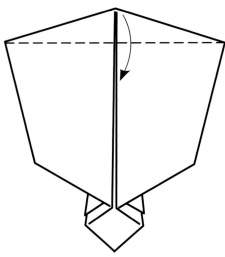

8. Fold the top point down.

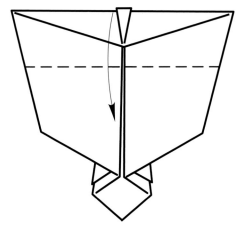

9. Valley fold downwards.

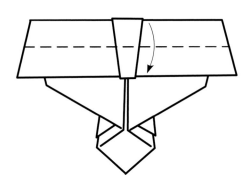

10. Valley fold in half.

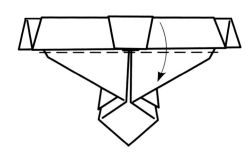

11. Fold the strip down.

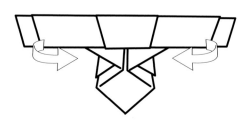

12. Curl the two strips around the bottle at a downward angle.

Moisten the strips where they cross over to fix them to the bottle.

Set your table with napkins held in this elegant and unusual napkin ring. Choose paper with contrasting colours on both sides.

Butterfly Napkin Ring

by Rikki Donachie

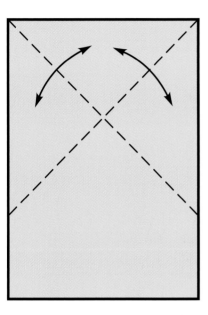

1. Begin with a sheet of A4 and fold the two diagonals.

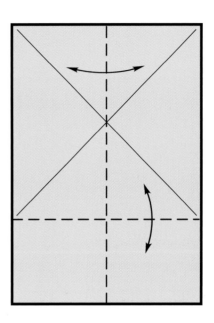

2. Fold in half vertically and fold up the bottom edge as shown.

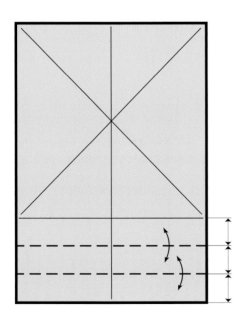

3. Divide the bottom rectangle into horizontal thirds.

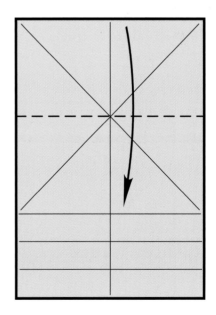

4. Valley fold the square in half downwards.

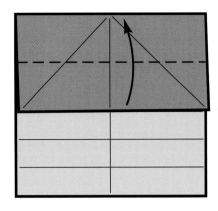

5. Valley fold upwards...

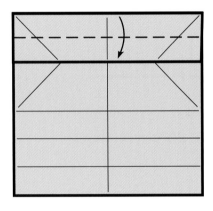

6. ...and downwards.

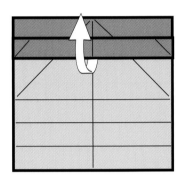

7. Unfold steps 4 and 5, leaving step 6 in place. - See next picture.

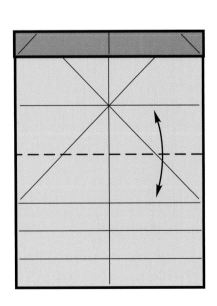

8. Valley crease.

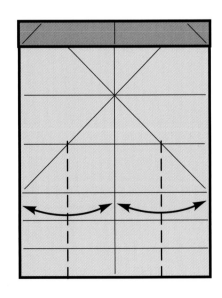

9. Valley creases.

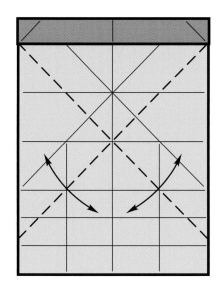

10. Valley creases.

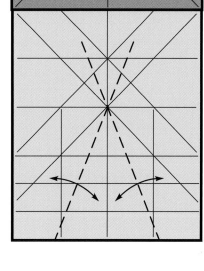

11. Valley creases.

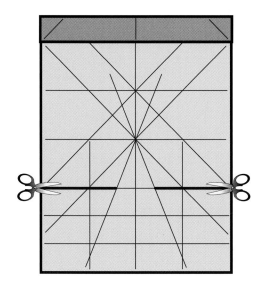

12. Cut along the creases where shown, making sure that you do not go further than the inner diagonal creases.

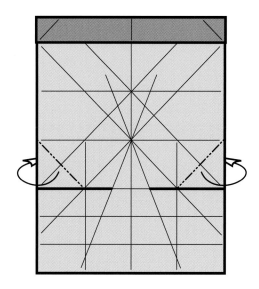

13. Mountain fold the indicated corners behind.

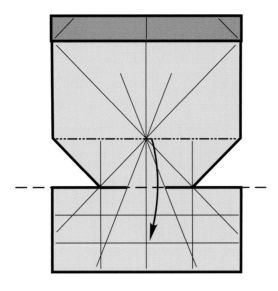

14. Zig-zag fold the top part down as shown.

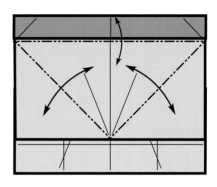

15. Place mountain creases where shown.

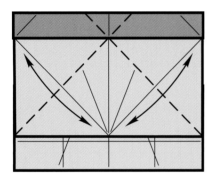

16. Valley crease two diagonals.

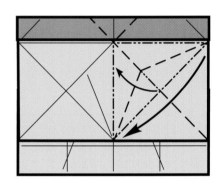

17. Using the creases made in steps 14 and 15, collapse one half of the paper. The next 2 pictures show the process.

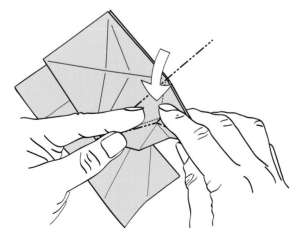

18. Sink the middle triangle like a rabbit's ear with both index fingers.

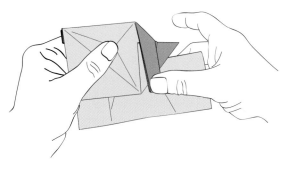

19. When sunk, flatten neatly and repeat steps 16-18 on the left-hand side.

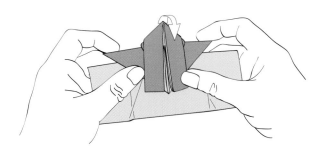

20. When both sides have been folded you will probably notice a little hood at the back of the top point. Bring this hood over to the front ...

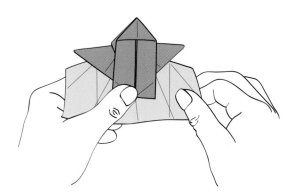

21. ...and flatten.

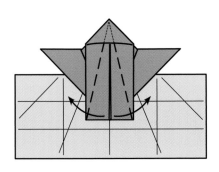

22. Valley fold the nearest layer out to reveal the wing colour.

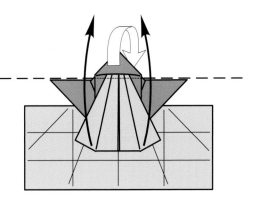

23. Lift up the bottom edges while allowing the little hood to fold down over the back.

49

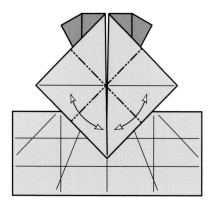

24. Mountain crease two diagonals as shown.

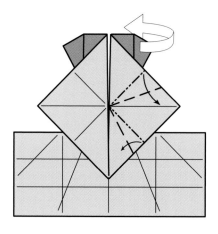

25. Fold the right-hand wings as shown. Make sure you start with the rear wing first and allow the top corner of the forewing to flip around.

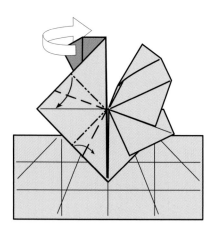

26. Repeat step 25 on the left-hand side.

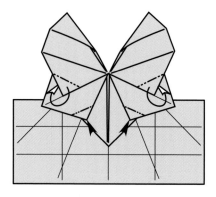

27. Mountain fold the forewings and sink the rear wings.

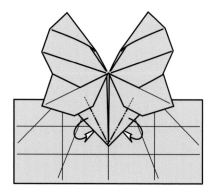

28. Narrow the abdomen.

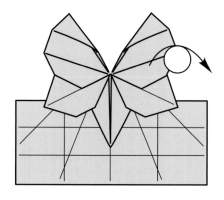

29. Turn the model over.

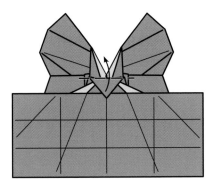

30. Lift the head.

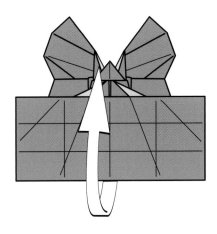

31. Lift up the bottom rectangle.

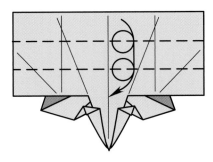

32. Fold the rectangle over and over on the previously made creases.

33. Bring the ends of the ring around and tuck one into the other.

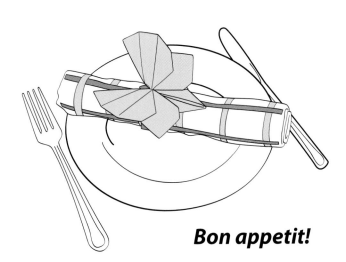

Bon appetit!

Curvy Bowl

An elegant and clever design of bowl or dish.
This design makes use of extensive precreasing before collapsing into the final shape with an ingenious lock.
Choose fairly thick and strong paper.

by David Mitchell

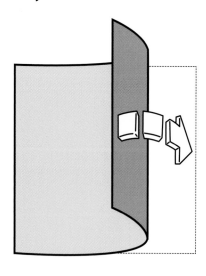

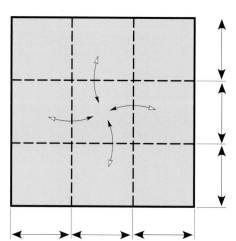

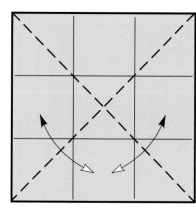

1. Lay the paper coloured side down.

2. Divide into horizontal and vertical thirds. (See page 5)

3. Valley crease diagonally.

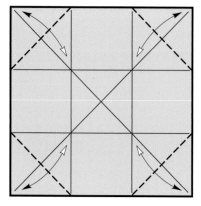

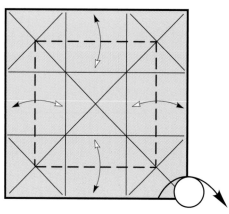

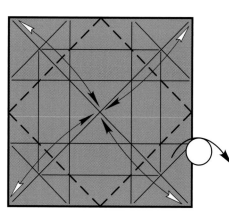

4. Valley crease the four corners as shown.

5. Valley crease in the middle of the four sides as shown.
Turn the paper over.

6. Fold and unfold all four corners to the centre.
Turn the paper over.

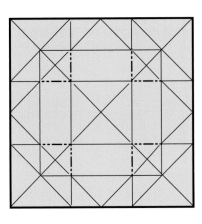

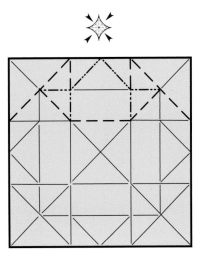

7. Reverse the crease segments as shown.

8. Gently collapse one edge of the paper as shown in Step 9.

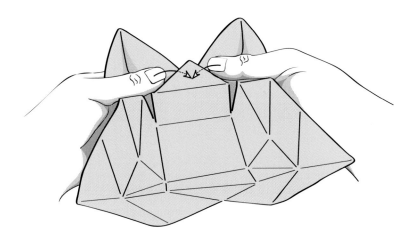

9. With the triangle pointing straight up, bring the two corners behind in the direction of the arrows.

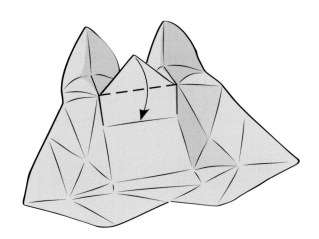

10. Swing the triangular flap down in front to create and lock one side of the bowl.

11. Step 8 completed.

The double dotted lines show where soft valley folds must be made to create curves in the edges of the finished bowl. Although there is insufficient tension in the other folds to hold these curves in place at the moment, it is a good idea to practise making them now so that you understand where they need to go. ***Remember they are soft folds. You should be very careful not to crease the paper as you make them.***

Look at Step 14 to see what the soft folds should look like from the outside.

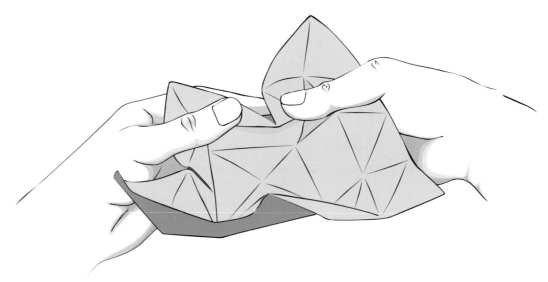

12. Turn the bowl counter-clockwise and collapse the second edge in the same way. The picture shows the collapse in progress. The edge you have already collapsed is on the left.

You will need to add the soft curves to both sides as you do this. The paper will hold its shape better this time.

Now collapse each of the remaining edges in turn in the same way. You may find the final collapse difficult to achieve, but persevere. It will be possible if you add the soft folds as you go.

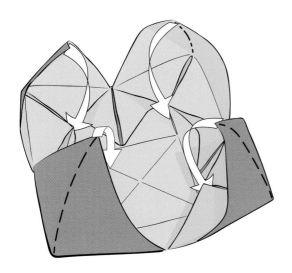

13. This is the result. To complete the bowl tuck the corners of the original square down into the pockets inside them. You will have to reverse the direction of the diagonal creases to achieve this.

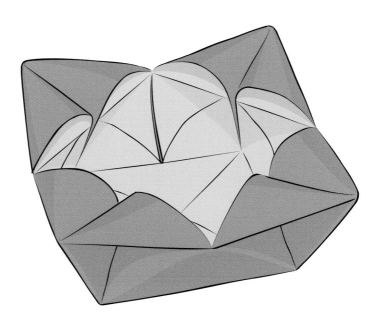

14. The finished bowl.
Ready for nuts, crisps or whatever you choose.

Origami You Can Use ...

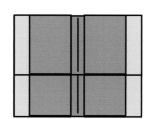

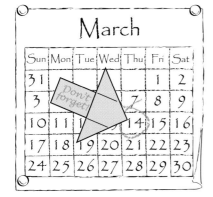

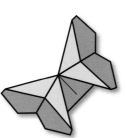

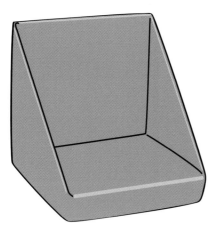

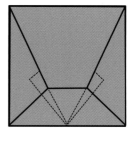

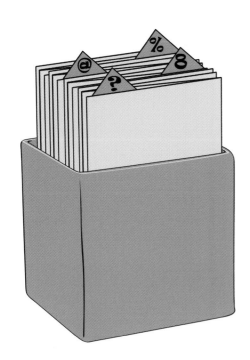

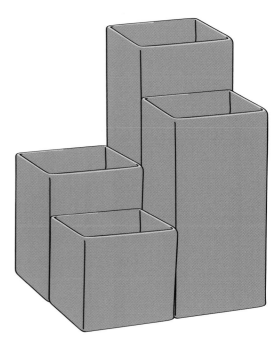

... at the Office ...

Fold your Post-it Notes into an arrow shape, which can then be positioned on a map, or index list so as to mark specific details; the address you will be going to can be written on the shaft of the arrow!

Begin by using a standard rectangular Post-it Note, carefully applying a cellophane strip to the gummed edge while folding, so that maximum stickiness is maintained until you're finished!

Post-it Note Arrow

by Rick Beech

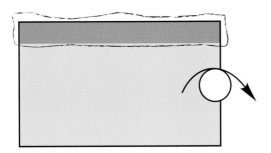

1. Place a strip of cellophane over the sticky edge, then turn over.

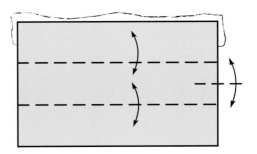

2. Divide into thirds (see page 5) and pinch the centre of the right-hand edge.

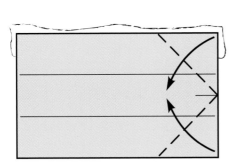

3. Valley fold the right-hand corners into the centre.

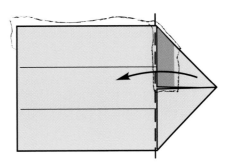

4. Valley fold the point over to the left.

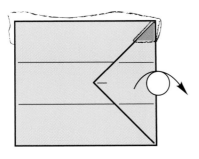

5. Turn the note over.

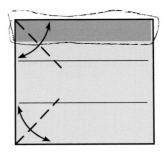

6. Valley crease as shown.

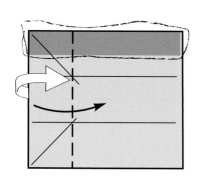

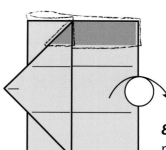

7. Valley fold the left-hand edge as shown, allowing the point to flip around.

8. Turn the note over.

9. Fold the edge up while squashing the right-hand corner.

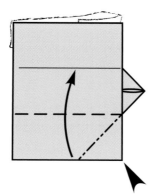

10. Repeat step 9 on the top edge.

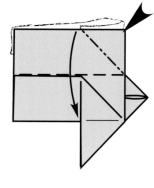

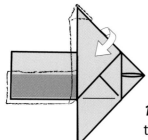

11. Bring the triangular flap to the front.

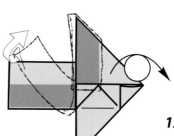

12. Remove the cellophane strip and stick the arrow where you want!

A simple and ingenious design capable of holding up to 10 business cards. Begin with a sheet of A4 paper.

Business Card Holder

by Larry Hart

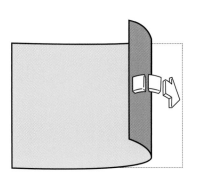

1. Lay the paper coloured side down.

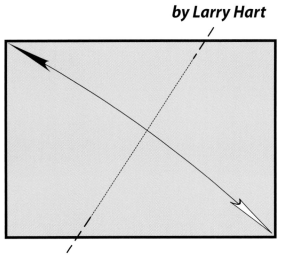

2. Bring opposite corners together and make small pinches on the edges of the paper.

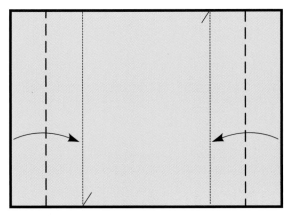

3. Valley fold the sides in to touch the pinches made in Step 2.

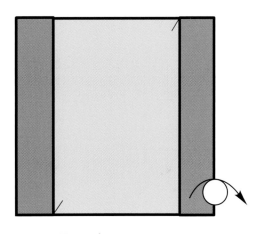

4. Turn the paper over.

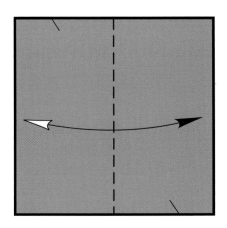

5. Valley crease vertically in half.

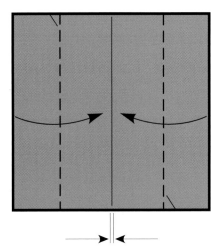

6. Valley fold the sides to the middle, leaving a 2 mm gap on either side of the central crease.

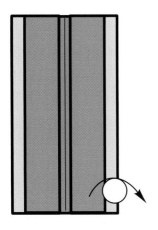

7. Turn the paper over.

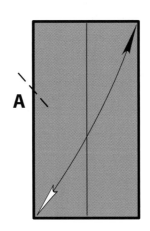

8. Bring opposite corners together and make a pinch on one side - Pinch A.

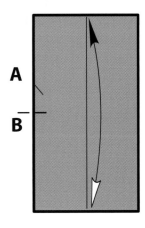

9. Make another pinch halfway down one side - Pinch B.

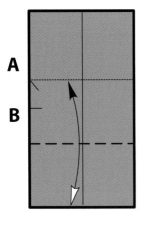

10. Bring the bottom edge to Pinch A and crease.

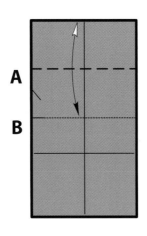

11. Bring the top edge to Pinch B and crease.

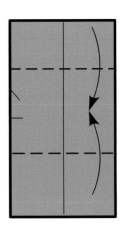

12. Remake folds 10 and 11 and tuck one end into the other.

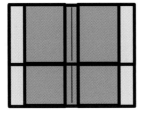

13. The finished Business Card Holder. This will also work with US Letter size paper.

This delightfully simple fold can be used just like a paper clip, as a bookmark or add an ingenious adornment to the corner of a letter!

Butterfly Page Corner

by Gay Merrill Gross, based on a model by Ralph Matthews

Duo paper, thin and crisp, works best for this design, which begins with paper in the proportion of 3:2 A handy size for a page is 2 ⅜" x 1 ⁹⁄₁₆" or 60 mm x 40 mm.

The paper should be placed with the wing-flash colour uppermost.

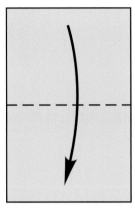

1. Fold paper in half downwards.

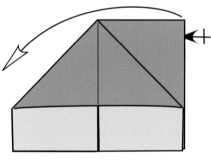

2. Fold in half from left to right.

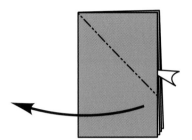

3. Lift the front flap over to the left and squash, see next picture for detail.

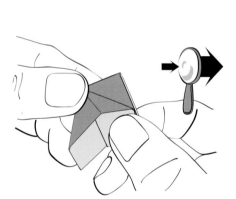

3a. Step 3 in progress.

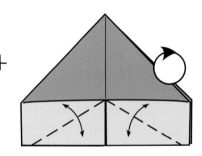

4. Repeat step 3 on the other side.

5. Precrease the lower flaps as shown.
Note that fold lines do **not** meet the outer corners.
Then rotate paper by 180°.

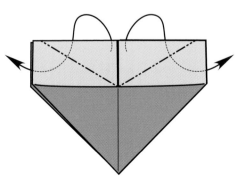

6. Inside reverse fold the two flaps, see next picture for details.

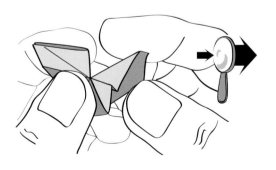

6a. Step 6 in progress.

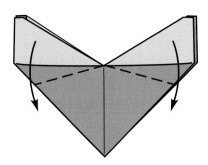

7. Valley fold the near flaps down at a slight angle.

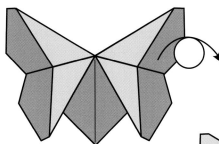

8. Turn butterfly over.

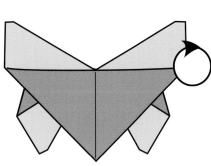

9. Rotate clockwise by 135°.

10. Slip the page or pages into the triangular pocket and valley fold the top left-hand corner as shown.

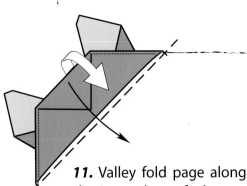

11. Valley fold page along the sloping edge of the pocket while allowing the butterfly to swing around to the front.

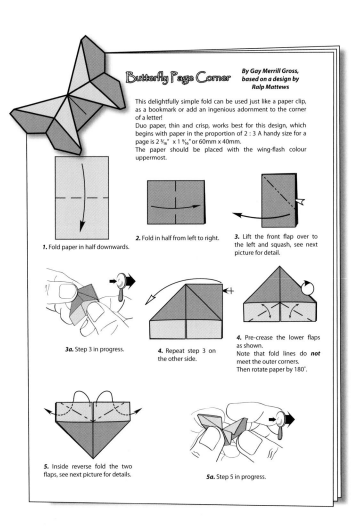

Butterfly Page Corner

By Gay Merrill Gross, based on a design by Ralp Mattews

This delightfully simple fold can be used just like a paper clip, as a bookmark or add an ingenious adornment to the corner of a letter!

Duo paper, thin and crisp, works best for this design, which begins with paper in the proportion of 2 : 3 A handy size for a page is 2 ³⁄₁₆" x 1 ⁹⁄₁₆" or 60mm x 40mm.

The paper should be placed with the wing-flash colour uppermost.

1. Fold paper in half downwards.

2. Fold in half from left to right.

3. Lift the front flap over to the left and squash, see next picture for detail.

3a. Step 3 in progress.

4. Repeat step 3 on the other side.

4. Pre-crease the lower flaps as shown.
Note that fold lines do **not** meet the outer corners.
Then rotate paper by 180°.

5. Inside reverse fold the two flaps, see next picture for details.

5a. Step 5 in progress.

12. Use the finished Butterfly Corner to keep important papers together.

This design is a simple holder for CDs. It has a rather stylish locking mechanism, and can be fashioned from pre-printed paper, so use your imagination!
You will require a sheet of sturdy European A4 or American letter paper, slight adjustments may be needed in each case. Begin with the printed / patterned side face down.

CD Wallet

by Rick Beech

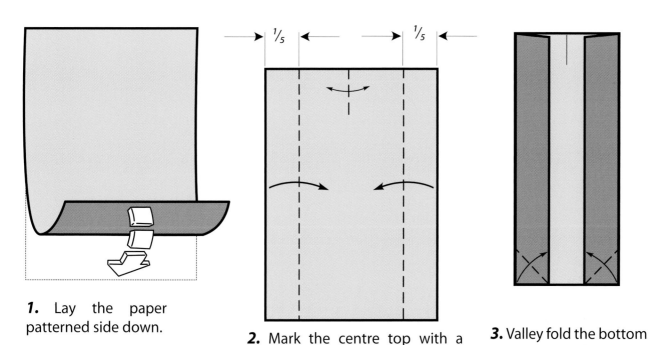

1. Lay the paper patterned side down.

2. Mark the centre top with a short crease and fold the sides in by 1/5th - see pages 6-7.

3. Valley fold the bottom corners up as shown.

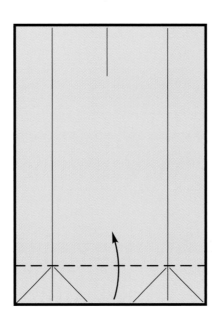

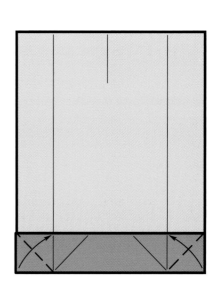

4. Open up everything back to a flat piece of paper.

5. Valley fold the bottom edge up as shown.

6. Valley fold the bottom corners in.

63

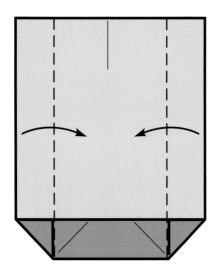

7. Valley fold the sides in.

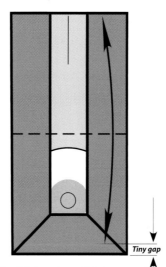

8. Slide the CD in and fold the top down so that there is a tiny gap between the bottom edges.

Tiny gap

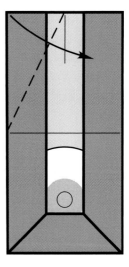

9. Valley fold the top left-hand corner over as shown.

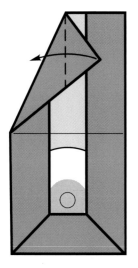

10. Valley fold the corner over to the left as shown.

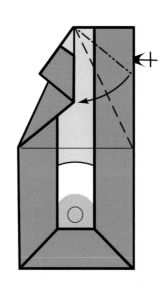

11. Repeat steps 9-10 on the right-hand side.

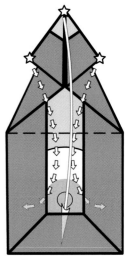

12. Fold the top down and tuck the 3 corners marked with stars under the flaps at the bottom.

13. The completed CD Wallet.

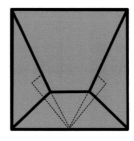

64

Nowadays it seems that we all have piles of CDs and CD-ROMs kicking around our desks. Fold this little shelf and tidy them all up into one place.
Use 120-150 gsm A2 paper.

CD Desk Rack

by Rikki Donachie

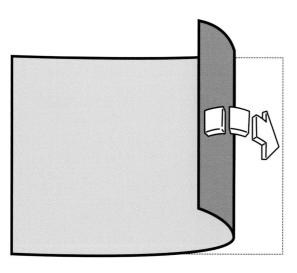

1. Lay paper coloured side down in landscape format.

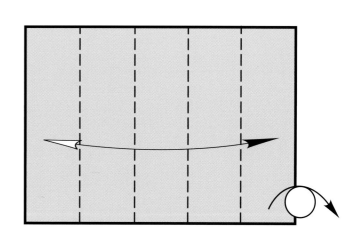

2. Divide into fifths. See page 6. Turn paper over.

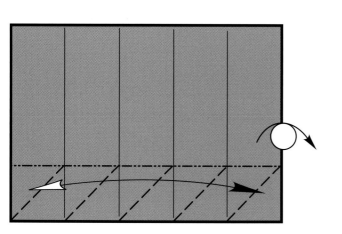

3. Valley fold diagonals at the bottom of each fifth and mountain fold across.
Turn the paper over.

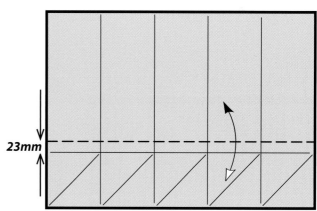

23mm

4. Valley fold horizontally 23 mm above the crease made in Step 3.

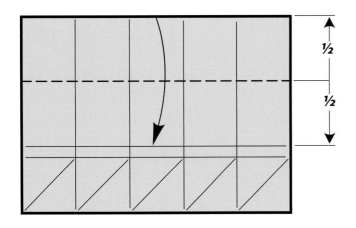

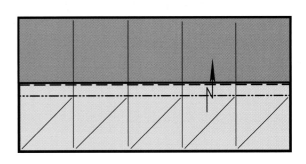

5. Valley fold the top edge down to just touch the crease made in Step 4.

6. Zig-zag fold upwards as shown.

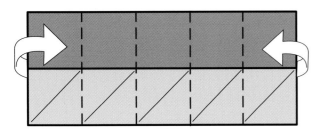

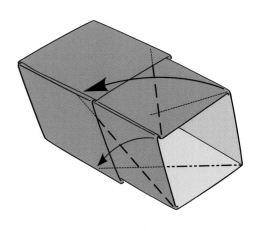

7. Curl the paper round to form a square cylinder, making sure that one end is tucked into the other neatly and fully.

8. Twist the bottom on the creases made in Step 3 while pushing in.

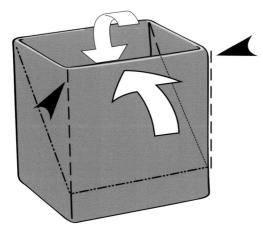

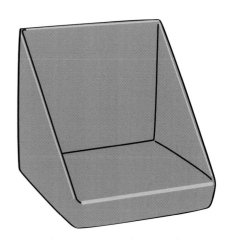

9. Push the front in as shown until it lies flat on the base. You will need to make diagonal mountains on each side and sink the nearside vertical edges with valley folds.

10. The finished CD Desk Rack. This will also hold A5 sized books.

With this desk tidy all those pots and jars full of pencils, pens, rulers and odd bits and bobs will be a thing of the past.
It is completely expandable and can be colour coordinated to suit your own tastes.
It uses the same folding sequence as the CD Desk Rack on page 65.
Choose 3 sheets of A3 paper that are about 150 gsm in weight.

Desk Tidy
by Rikki Donachie

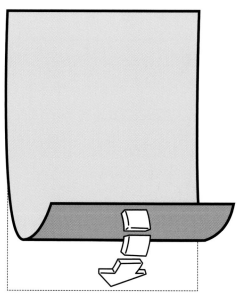

1. Start with one of the sheets of A3 and lay it coloured side down in portrait format.

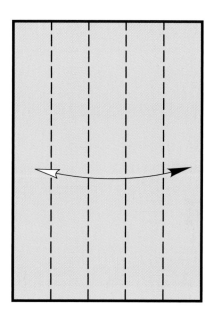

2. Divide into vertical fifths. See page 6.

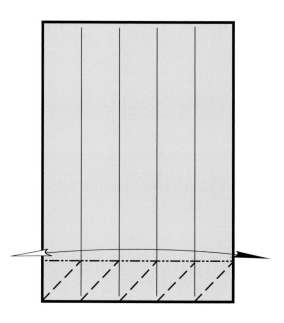

3. Put in diagonal valley folds across the bottom of each panel and a horizontal mountain fold as shown.

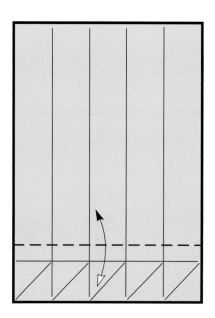

4. Valley crease approximately 10 mm above the mountain crease made in Step 3.

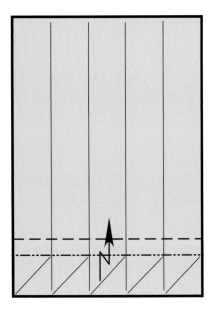

5. Zig-zag fold on the creases made in Steps 3 and 4.

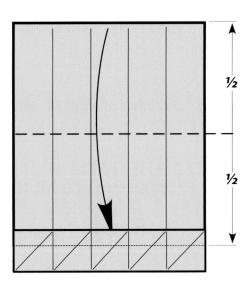

6. Valley fold the top edge down all the way to touch the valley fold made in Step 4.

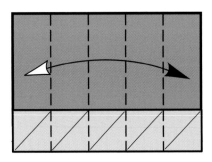

7. Re-crease the verticals as valley folds.

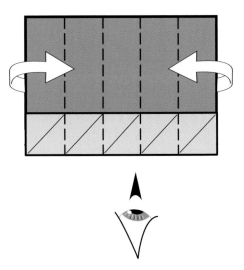

8. Wrap the paper around to form a square cylinder, making sure that it is all tucked in tightly and correctly.
The next step is viewed from underneath.

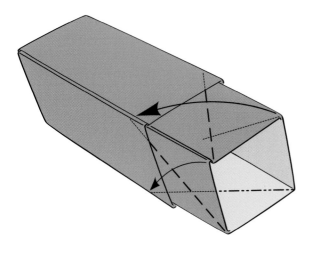

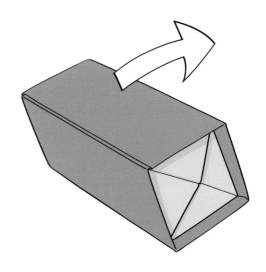

9. Twist the base on the diagonal creases and push in towards the rest of the unit.

10. The base of the box should look like this.
Bring the unit to the vertical.

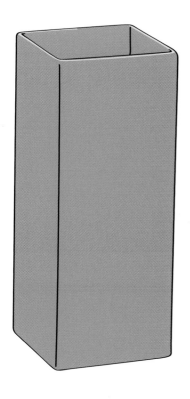

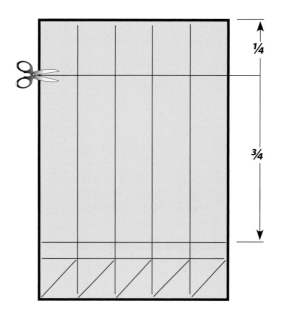

11. One section of the desk tidy.

12. With the second sheet of A3 complete Steps 1-4 and then cut off a strip as shown. Complete by folding Steps 5- 9.
This will give a unit slightly shorter than the first one.

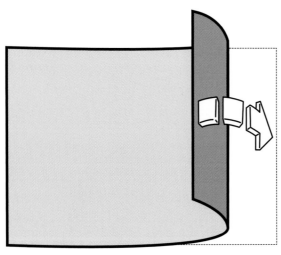

13. Take the third sheet of A3 and cut in half. Producing two sheets of A4. Lay one sheet coloured side down in landscape format.

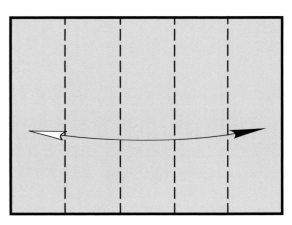

14. Crease into vertical fifths. See page 6.

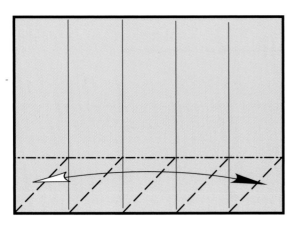

15. Repeat Step 3 across the bottom edge.

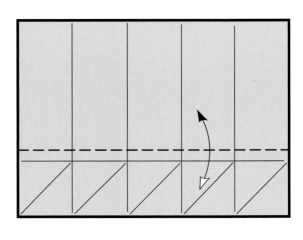

16. Repeat Step 4 across the bottom edge.

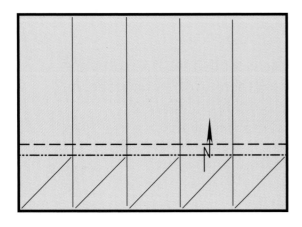

17. After zig-zag folding as in Step 5. Repeat Steps 6-10 to form the unit.

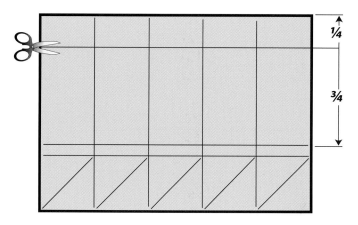

18. With the second sheet of A4 complete Steps 13-16 and then cut off a strip as shown. Complete by folding Step 17. This will give a unit slightly shorter than the first one.

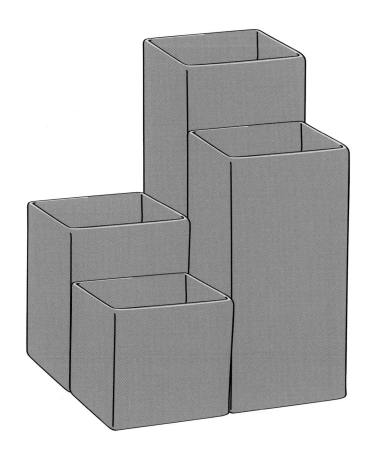

19. The four units can be easily fixed together with double sided sticky tape.
Adjust the relative heights to taste and add more units as and when you feel like it.

Map Fold

by Rikki Donachie

This is a very simple but effective way to fold a large sheet of paper in such a way that it can be unfolded to its full extent in one easy move and collapsed just as easily.

The diagrams that follow should be viewed with the printed side that you wish to read as the coloured side.

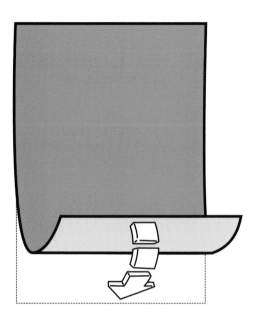

1. Lay the paper printed side up.

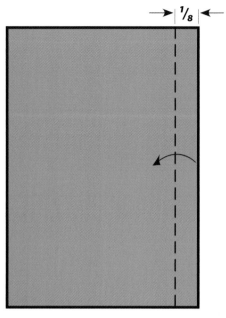

2. Valley fold the right-hand side in by $\frac{1}{8}$ of the width.

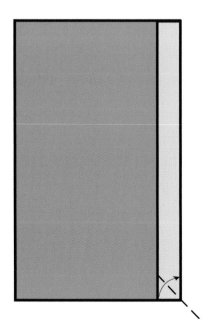

3. Valley fold the bottom corner up.

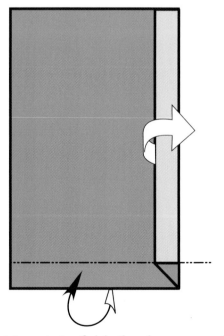

4. Mountain fold the bottom edge behind.
Then unfold everything .

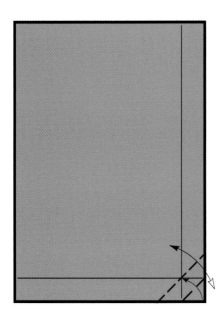

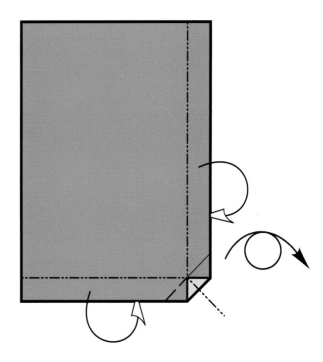

5. Valley fold the bottom corner to the crease intersection.
Valley crease through the intersection at 45°.

6. Mountain fold on both indicated creases while pinching the bottom corner as shown.
Turn the paper over.

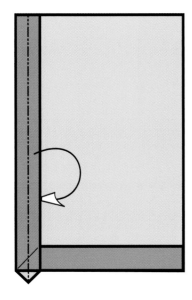

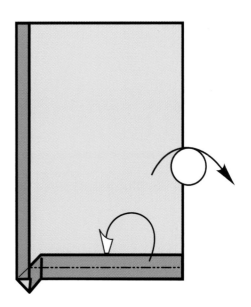

7. Ensure the paper looks like the drawing.
Mountain fold the left side under as shown.

8. Mountain fold the bottom edge as shown.
Turn the paper over.

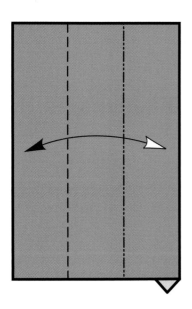

9. Zig-zag fold and unfold into vertical thirds as shown.
To fold into thirds see page 5.

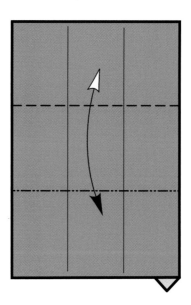

10. Zig-zag fold and unfold into horizontal thirds as shown.
To fold into thirds see page 5.

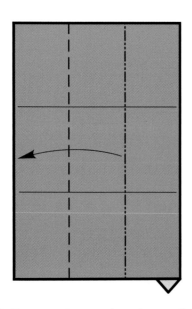

11. Repeat Step 9 but leave folded.

12. Repeat Step 10 but leave folded.

13. The completed Map Fold in its collapsed state.

14. If, like me, you cannot survive without a pocket diary, but also find it tricky to see the tiny print on occasions. Try this;
Glue the collapsed Map Fold to the inside cover of your diary.
That's it!

15. Pull on the little tab and it will open out. It will fold itself back up just by pushing the tab back towards its original position.

Note. This folding sequence will work for any rectangle. "A" proportions are particularly good because they will reduce down to "A" proportions.

If you wish to reduce a very large sheet down to a very small size, divide the horizontals and/or the verticals into fifths or even sevenths.

Any odd number above 1 will work as long as the top horizontal fold and the left-hand vertical fold are **both valleys** and then alternate subsequent parallel folds mountain-valley-mountain.

Mini Filing Cabinet

by Rikki Donachie

In origami it is common to combine two different designs together in order to produce a third.
This design combines the Map Fold with the CD Desk Rack to produce a Filing Cabinet small enough to carry around with you. Unlike a laptop computer it will never need recharging.

Choose A4 paper for both the box and the files.

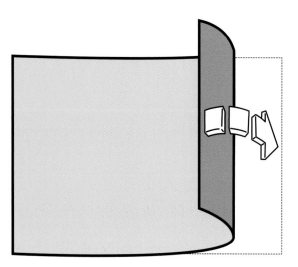

1. Lay paper coloured side down in landscape format.

2. Repeat Steps 2 - 8 of the CD Desk Rack. Page 65.

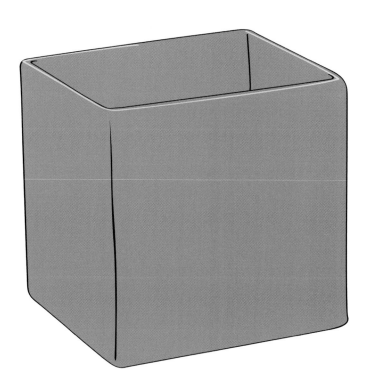

3. The finished box awaiting its files.

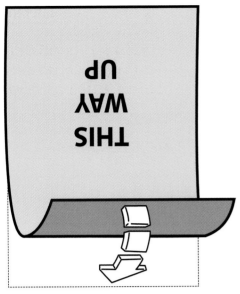

4. Lay the file paper printed side up but otherwise upside down. See picture.

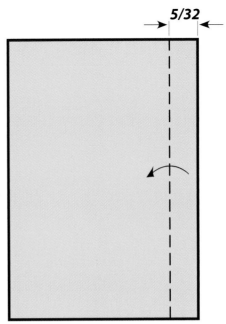

5. Valley fold the right-hand edge in by $^5/_{32}$ of the total width.
To put the tab on the other edge of the paper, fold the left-hand edge by the same amount instead.

6. Repeat Steps 3 -12 of the Map Fold. Page 72.

7. Label the tabs to taste.

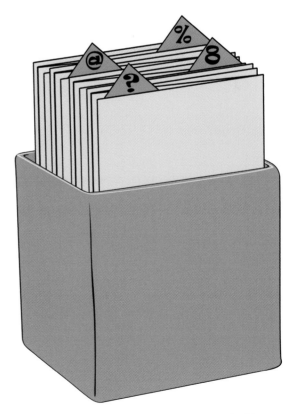

8. The completed Mini Filing Cabinet with files.

Origami You Can Use ...

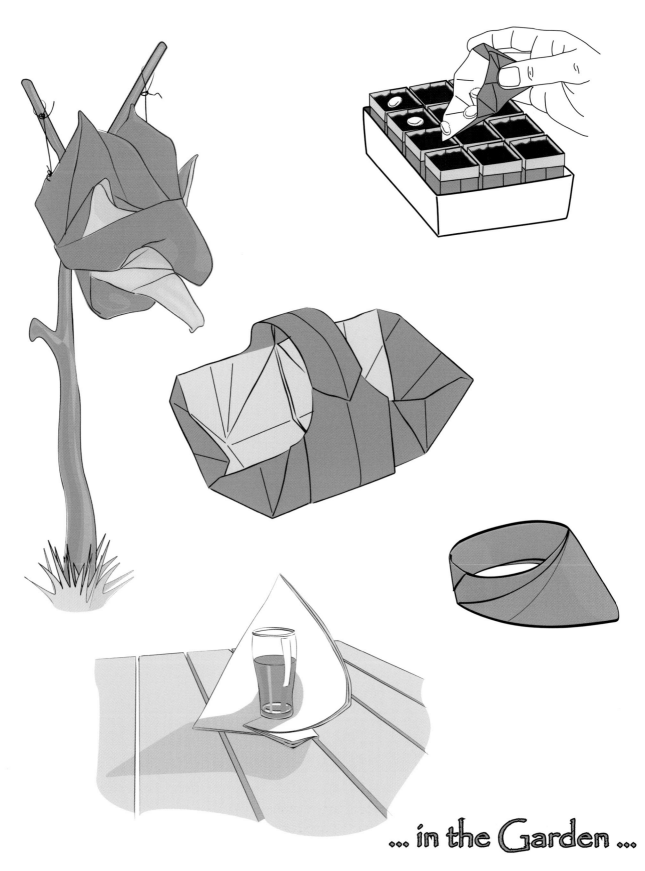

... in the Garden ...

For all keen gardeners. A perfect little envelope for collecting your own seeds in. It can be locked shut and has a neat funnel for sowing the seeds in springtime.

Seed Packet

by Rikki Donachie

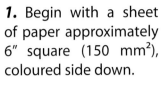

1. Begin with a sheet of paper approximately 6" square (150 mm²), coloured side down.

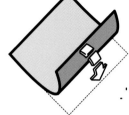

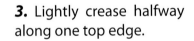

2. Valley crease vertically.

3. Lightly crease halfway along one top edge.

½ ½

4. Valley fold the left-hand corner over to just touch the crease made in step 2.

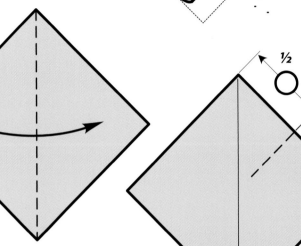

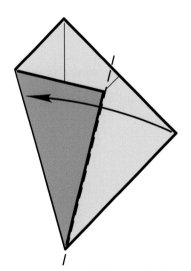

5. Valley fold the right-hand corner over to meet the left-hand edge.

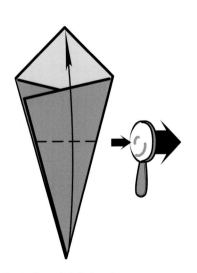

6. Valley fold the bottom corner up to meet the top corner.

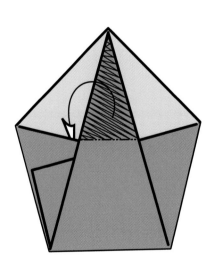

7. Tuck the shaded triangle down inside the envelope.

79

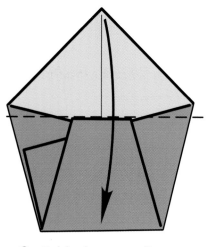

8. Fold the top flap down as shown.

9. Inside reverse fold each corner underneath the front sloping edges. See step 9a.

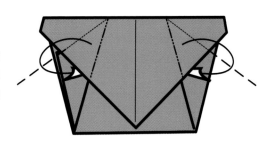

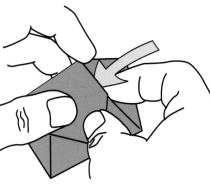

9a. Hold the packet as shown and use your index finger to push the sides underneath the sloping edge in the direction of the red arrow. Then repeat with the other corner.

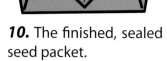

Delphinium
9th June 2008

10. The finished, sealed seed packet.
Don't forget to record what the seeds are and the date of harvest.

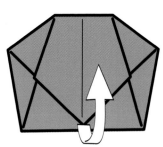

11. Lift the flap, fill with freshly gathered seeds and repeat steps 8 - 10 to seal the envelope. When it comes time to sow the seed, just lift the flap...

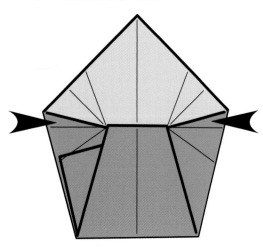

12. ...squeeze the sides...

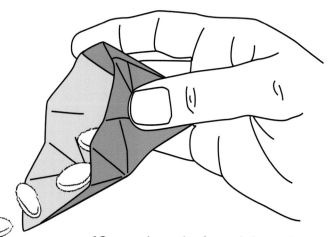

13. ...and use the funnel shaped flap to guide the seeds in a controlled manner.

This little seedling pot is ideal for sowing one or two seeds in and, when the plantlets are sufficiently large, the entire pot can be planted out into the garden - the paper of the pot will slowly decompose into the soil.

Seedling Pot

by Rikki Donachie

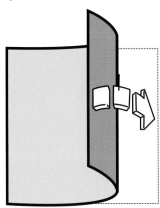

1. Begin with a sheet of paper approximately 8″ square (210 mm²), coloured side down.

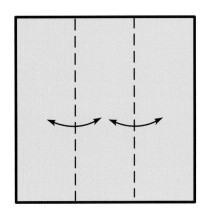

2. Divide into thirds vertically (see page 5).

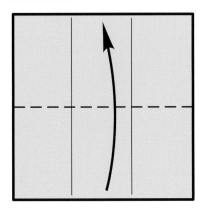

3. Valley fold bottom edge up to the top.

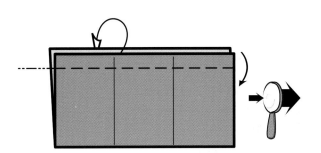

4. Valley fold approximately ½″ (12 mm) down in front and behind.

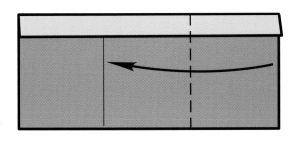

5. Valley fold the right-hand third across.

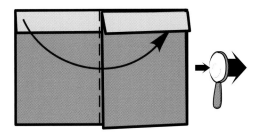

6. Valley fold the left-hand third over and tuck under the overhang made in step 4.

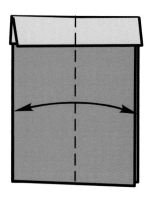 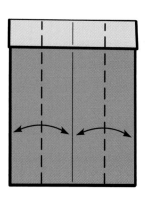 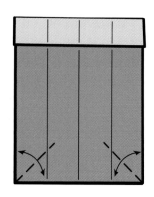 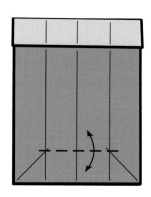

7. Precrease firmly with valley **and** mountain folds.

8. Precrease firmly with valley **and** mountain folds.

9. Precrease firmly with valley **and** mountain folds.

10. Precrease firmly with valley **and** mountain folds.

11a. Looking from the top, separate the 3 thin edges from the single thick edge to form a cylinder with a base.

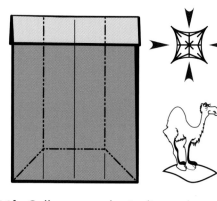

11b. Collapse on the indicated mountain folds to form the 3-D square cylinder shape.

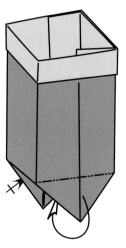

12. Fold the triangular corners under and shape the pot.

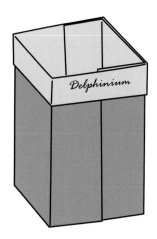

13. The finished pot. Write the name of the seeds on the top edge.

Delphinium

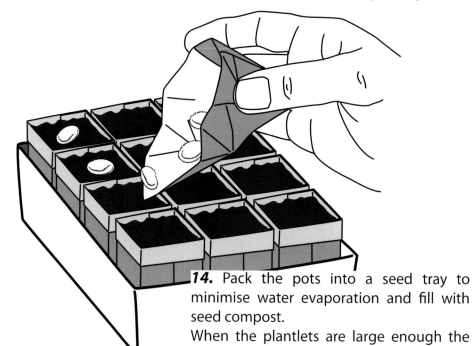

14. Pack the pots into a seed tray to minimise water evaporation and fill with seed compost.
When the plantlets are large enough the entire pot can be planted into the soil.

After collecting your seeds and sowing them into the little pots it will soon be time to plant them out into the garden. To keep hungry birds away from your tender young seedlings, fold this fun bird scarer.

Glue holographic foil paper to strong contrasting paper for the best effect. After folding the mask brush on 2 or 3 coats of yacht grade varnish or dilute PVA (polyvinyl adhesive) to make it waterproof. (See page 93.)

Bird Scarer

by Rikki Donachie

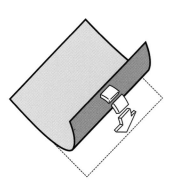

1. After preparing the paper, lay it coloured side down.

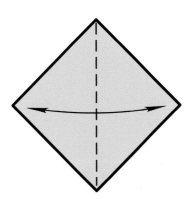

2. Valley crease on the vertical diagonal.

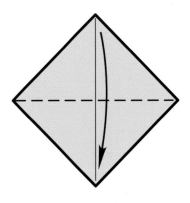

3. Valley fold on the horizontal diagonal.

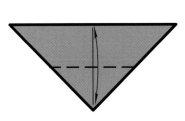

4. Lift the bottom corner to the top edge and crease. Unfold.

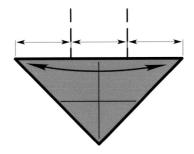

5. Divide the top edge into thirds. See page 5.

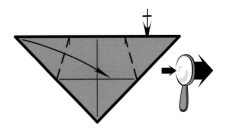

6. Valley fold the corners in using the creases made in Steps 4 and 5 as a guide.

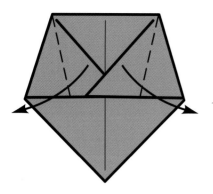

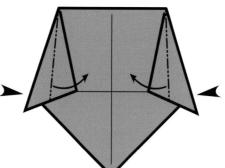

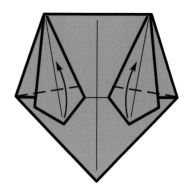

7. Valley fold both flaps outwards.

8. Lift and squash both side flaps.

9. Valley fold the bottom corner of each flap upwards at the angle shown.

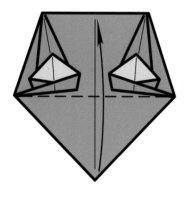

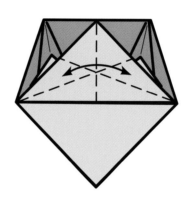

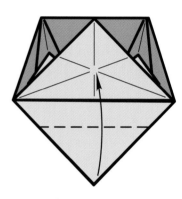

10. Valley fold the bottom corner up as far as it will comfortably go.

11. Precrease the upper triangle by bisecting each corner.

12. Bring the bottom corner up to touch the intersection of the creases made in Step 11.

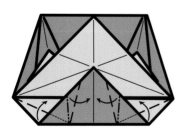

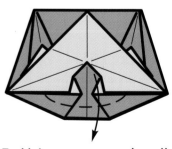

13. Shape the tongue by making the folds as shown.

14. From this point on the model will not lie flat.

15. Using a curved valley fold bring the tongue down and forwards.

84

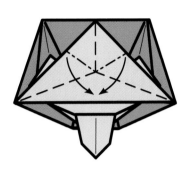

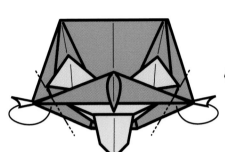

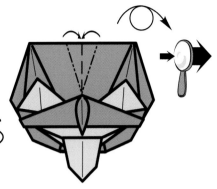

16. Form the nose as shown.

17. Mountain fold the sides behind at an angle.

18. Shape the whole face by putting in an inside reverse fold at the top. The wider the angle between the mountain folds the more curved the face will be.
Turn the mask over.

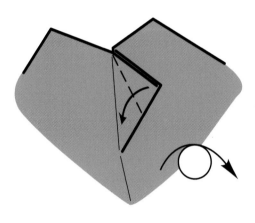

19. Close up of the reverse fold made in Step 18.
To lock the fold in place valley fold the tip down as shown and flatten against the back of the mask.
Turn over.

20. From this point on all the shaping and modelling is done.
Slightly dampen the paper and mould and shape the mask to your own taste. Allowing each part to dry before moving onto the next. Clothes pins can be useful third and fourth hands.
Once it moulded to your satisfaction brush on 2 or 3 coats of dilute PVA to weatherproof it. (See page 93.)

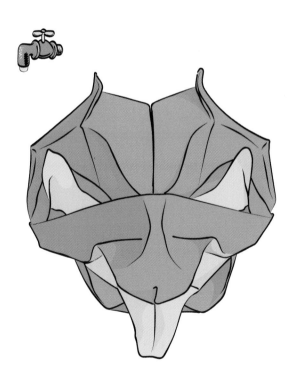

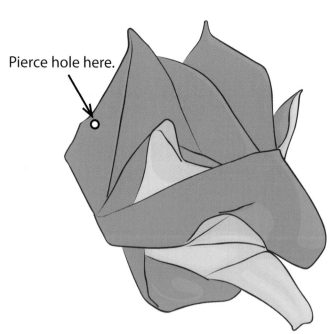

Pierce hole here.

21. Once the PVA is dry make two holes on either side at the back of the mask and thread string through them.

Tie the mask to a forked stick and insert into your freshly sown seedbed.

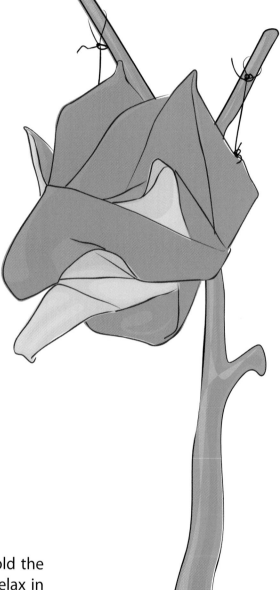

22. The finished bird scarer.

After all of that work you deserve to fold the Sun Visor and Patent Beer Shade and relax in your garden...

The authors have known this design for some years. Unfortunately we do not know who created it. We have searched the Internet and asked around the origami community, all to no avail. So, if you have met this design before and you know who created it, please let us know.

Basket

The design is surprisingly strong and hard wearing. Use it to collect fresh vegetables or flowers from your garden (*I have easily carried up to 10Kg - RD*).

Choose paper of approximately 100 - 150 gsm and 600 mm² - 24". Hand made paper which usually has long fibres in it is very good. If you plan to reuse a number of times it would be worth pretreating the paper with PVA. (See page 93.)

by Unknown Creator

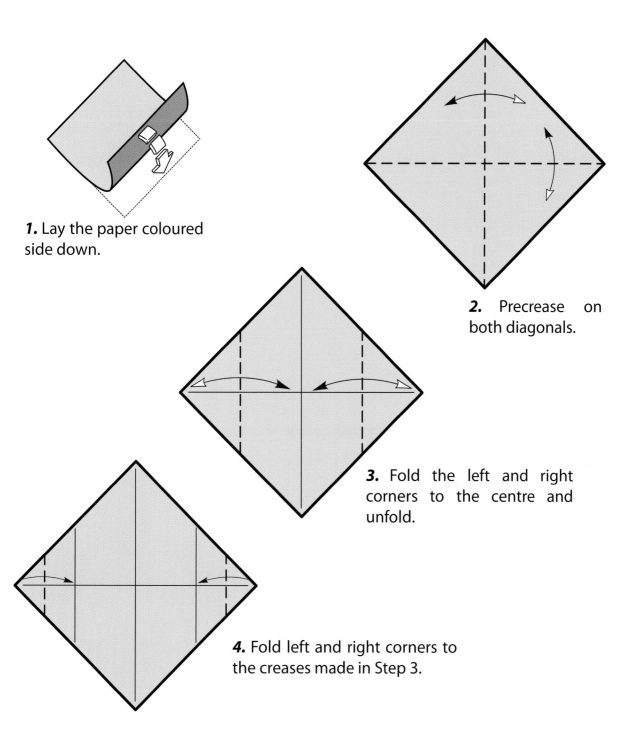

1. Lay the paper coloured side down.

2. Precrease on both diagonals.

3. Fold the left and right corners to the centre and unfold.

4. Fold left and right corners to the creases made in Step 3.

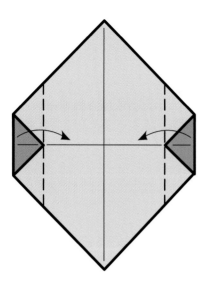

5. Fold in both side as shown.

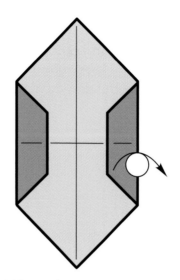

6. Turn the paper over.

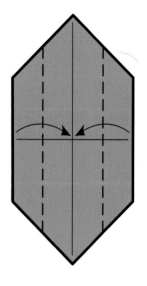

7. Fold both sides into the middle.

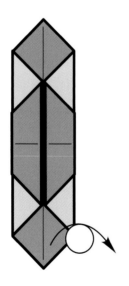

8. Turn the paper over.

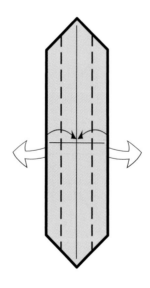

9. Fold the sides into the middle allowing the flaps at the back to swing out.

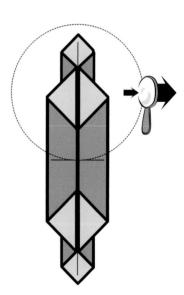

10. The next 3 steps focus on one end - Repeat each step at both ends.

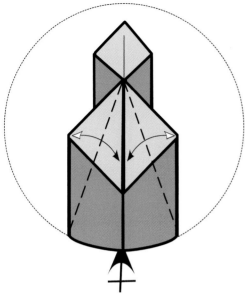

11. Valley crease the sloping sides into the middle.
Repeat at other end.

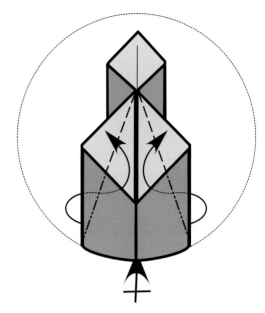

12. Using the creases made in Step 11, inside reverse fold both sides.
Repeat at other end.

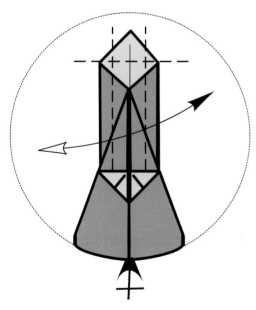

13. Valley crease the tip as shown. Repeat at other end, leaving one tip folded over (See next picture).

This tip has been left folded down. ➞

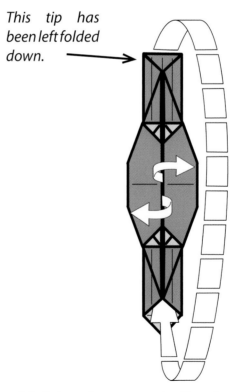

14. Bring the squared off end around and tuck it into the other end. While this is being done, open up the middle flaps and pull apart.

15. With the basket roughly shaped, mountain fold both sides of the handle over on the creases made in Step 13.

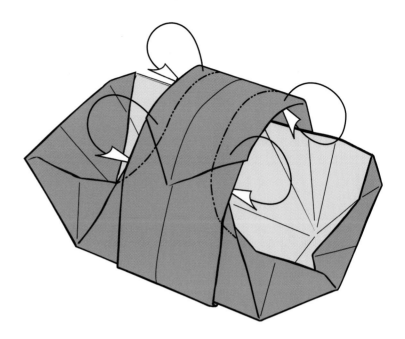

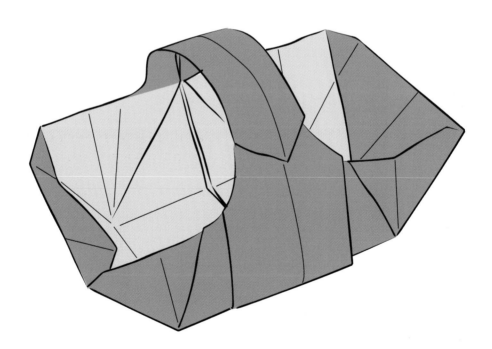

16. The basket is now ready for your freshly harvested vegetables.

Use a large square of sturdy, bright-coloured craft paper. A 60 cm square is ideal for an adult, try experimenting with a 40 - 45 cm size square for a child's visor. The model requires a little careful shaping in conclusion. Begin with the outer patterned side face down.
Be careful - paper can ignite in extreme heat! Ideally weatherproof with PVA, see page 93.

Sun Visor

by Rick Beech

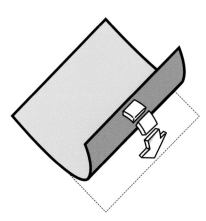

1. Place the paper coloured side down.

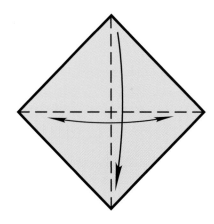

2. Crease both diagonals.

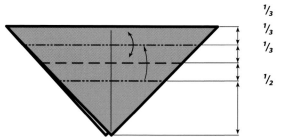

3. Precrease as shown. Then bring the bottom mountain fold up to the top crease.

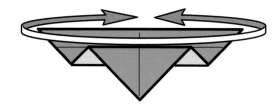

4. Bring the sides around and overlap them slightly to fit the head.

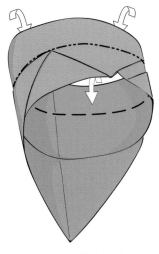

5. Mountain fold the top edge inside using the top mountain crease made in step 3.

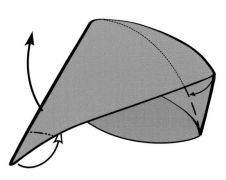

6. Swing the peak up. Note the valley fold.
Then fold over the tip.

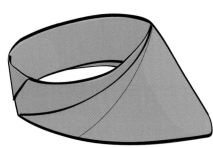

7. The finished sun visor.

Patent Beer Shade

by Rikki Donachie

Not only is this a very useful piece of origami, it is also one of the simplest. This was actually invented on a long, hot, sunny afternoon in the beer garden of my local pub and has been thoroughly tested. Any sized newspaper will do, although tabloid size is best.

1. Ensure that you have read everything you want to before folding.
Swing the lower right-hand corner over towards the left as shown.

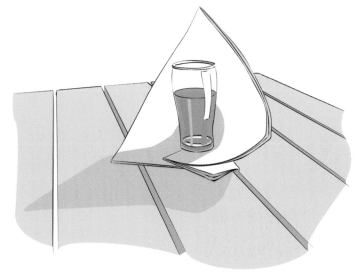

2. Place your glass of beer on the bottom to hold it down and turn the shade to block the sun.
Cheers!

Treating Paper with PVA

by Rikki Donachie

Paper that is used for practical purposes needs to be tough and hard wearing. Sometimes also wind and weather proof, attributes not often associated with paper. However, we can toughen paper up by a considerable amount if we pretreat it with PVA.

Materials and Equipment Required

PVA (polyvinyl adhesive). Also known as "White Glue". Buy a large tub from DIY or hardware stores. It is very much cheaper than the little pots available at art suppliers.

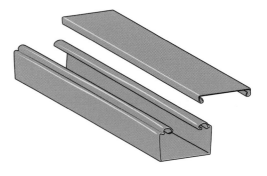

Plastic electrical cable trunking. The type that snaps together. This should be available at the same places as the PVA.

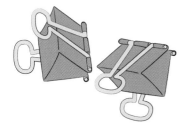

"Bulldog" clips or similar spring paper clips. Ordinary paper clips, one for each Bulldog. From any stationery shop.

An empty and clean plastic margarine/ice cream tub.

Clean paint brush - 1"-2" wide.

A large sheet of heavyweight polythene (available at the same place as the PVA or larger art supply stores. Heavyweight garden refuse sacks are suitable.)

Loads of old newspapers.

An indoor washing line where you can hang the wet paper overnight, free from disturbance and dust.

Method

1. Dilute the PVA. Put a few spoonfuls of PVA into the plastic tub and add cold water, stirring constantly until the mixture is the same consistency as milk. Make sure that it is thoroughly mixed. The unmixed PVA has a tendency to hide in the corners of the tub.

2. Spread sheets of newspaper on the floor and lay the heavyweight polythene sheet on top. This can be a little messy so make sure that the newspaper extends well beyond the edges of the polythene sheet.

3. Lay the sheet of paper to be treated on top of the polythene sheet. Ensuring that there is space all the way around it to the edges of the polythene.

4. Brush the diluted PVA solution onto the paper. Starting with the edge furthest away from you. Try to spread the solution as evenly as possible.

5. Turn the paper over. To do this easily and without ripping the paper, slide one half of the cable trunking underneath the edge of the paper and gently place the other half on top. Smooth sides together. Grip them together and lift the paper carefully. Turn the paper around and lay it back on the plastic. If the paper is very thin, omit this step.

6. Brush the PVA solution evenly onto the other side of the paper. Again starting with the edge furthest away from you.

7. Slide one half of the trunking underneath the edge of the paper and lay the other half on top, smooth sides together. Take 2 Bulldog clips and attach them to both parts of the trunking, evenly spaced apart. Attach a paper clip to each Bulldog clip.

8. Pick up the treated paper and, using the paper clips, hang it on the line. The paper will dry overnight and, because you have used plastic trunking, will not stick to the Bulldog clips or line. The combination of clips and trunking help to spread the load of the wet paper ensuring that it will dry evenly with few, if any, buckles.

9. When you have finished, clean everything thoroughly, paying special attention to the brush. The dilute solution will keep for some time if the lid has been securely attached to the tub, although it will settle out slightly and need a good stir before using it again.

NOTES

Handmade papers are the best to use as they have substantially longer fibres than commercial machine made paper.

If you wish to have different colours on either side of the paper, treat 2 sheets separately and then laminate them together once they are both dry.

Some papers have very water soluble dyes in them. This will colour the PVA solution.